Rotisserie Chicken Queen: 50 Fabulous Recipes That Start With Rotisserie Chicken

Plus, 7 Sensational Desserts

RECIPE PUBLISHERS
610 N. Elmwood Avenue
Springfield, Missouri 65802
www.RecipePubs.com

Copyright © 2015 by Juliana Goodwin

Library of Congress Control Number: 2015953086

ISBN: 978-0-9898137-6-1

Cover Design: John Cazort

Photography by: Juliana Goodwin

Publication Production: JE Cornwell

Printed in USA

Introduction

Before I had a child, rotisserie chicken was hardly ever on my table. I was a professional food writer with a weekly column in the Springfield News-Leader, and cooking was sacred to me.

In August, 2012, my baby Isabella Caroline was born and everything changed.

Time was precious. Dinner was daunting.

And the rotisserie chicken became my best mealtime friend. I bought at least two a week and made quick sides to doctor up the dinner. Being a busy mom, dinner was not the only meal I had to worry about. I had to pack lunch for myself and my daughter every day, and I wanted quick and healthy options.

These birds are easy, inexpensive and versatile. It's less expensive to buy a rotisserie chicken than to roast your own.

I can't get enough of them.

When I initially started buying these birds, it seemed like a healthier alternative to fast food and a lot less expensive than take out. Then, I started using the chicken to simplify dishes I already had in my repertoire. With my passion for food and cooking, it was only natural that I realized the potential for a rotisserie chicken cookbook and began cultivating recipes.

Soon, I realized the chicken could be used as a time saver in gumbo and many other recipes. In addition, rotisserie leftovers were perfect in sandwiches and added protein to salads.

Most of my recipes can be completed in 20-30 minutes. There are a few recipes that take more time, like my restaurant-quality Southwest Egg Rolls, but the grocery store bird still shaves off cooking time and simplifies the recipe.

On a cold winter day, make something comforting like my Pot Pie with Refrigerator Biscuits; Quick Posole; or Light, Chicken and Corn Chowder.

If you're entertaining, whip up my killer Buffalo Chicken Pizza (perfect for football season); or my Chicken, Andouille Po' Boy with Horseradish Slaw (so good you'll eat until you're miserable).

My Mexican Lasagna is one of my most popular recipes and it will feed a hungry family or a house full of guests. It freezes well, too.

In this book, I will prove rotisserie chicken can be transformed into a sophisticated meal like Quick Chicken Marsala or BLT Alfredo. Yes, you can seriously make all those dishes in 30 minutes or less using rotisserie chicken and each one is delicious. *Continued on next page*

Another beauty of these chickens is you can boil the carcasses and make stock. I can't tell you the last time I bought stock because I always make my own and freeze it. This is a money saver for sure. Every weekend, while I do laundry, I have a stock pot going filled with chicken, carrots, celery, onion, and bay leaves. Sometimes I add dried mushrooms and parsley. The house smells divine.

In the past year, I've also come up with a slow cooker stock which is incredibly easy (although a stovetop stock will always have a slightly richer flavor).

Over the years, I received two consistent compliments from my readers: they said they loved my recipes because the food was simple and delicious; I am also the queen of "tips" for using left-overs or repurposing a recipe. I offer similar tips throughout the book.

I consider it an honor to share recipes that people make for their family. Every single one of these dishes has been consumed by my family. These are my 50 best. I hope you enjoy them.

Tips for Working with Rotisserie Chicken:

Depending on where you buy it, a rotisserie chicken should yield 4 cups of chopped meat. SAMS Club has the plumpest birds which might give you a little more meat.

When you buy a bird, store it in the refrigerator within an hour of purchase to keep it fresh.

Some stores sell cold birds at a discounted price; be sure to check the "packaged on" and "sell by" date on those if you're not consuming it that day.

As a rule, if I buy a fresh bird, I will use the meat for up to 5 days (usually 4 to be on the safe side). But if I buy a refrigerated bird, which means it is already at least one day old, I will consume it within 3 days.

In handling hundreds of chickens, I've found the best way to shred the meat is to simply do it with your hands. I tear it off and hand shred it or then chop it, depending on what I need for the recipe.

As I mentioned, I use the carcass to make stock which saves me money and gives the bird another purpose. See my soup chapter for stock recipes.

You can freeze a rotisserie chicken, but it does change the texture of the meat, so I only recommend that for soup and casserole recipes.

Thank You

The night before my cookbook was due to the publisher, I went for a long walk about thought about how excited and blessed I was to be alive and about to accomplish this goal.

Writing a cookbook has been a dream of mine for many years and it's finally come true.

I could not have achieved this if it wasn't for my parents. From an early age, they nurtured my creativity and passions. From making mud pies when I was 3, to cooking my first burger when I was 6, I have always loved creating recipes. They have encouraged me every step of the way.

My mother is my biggest fan which I always appreciated, but now that I am a mom I truly understand how much it shaped me. I hope to be that same influence for my daughter. I am eternally thankful for their love and support.

I owe a big thank you to my husband who has eaten more rotisserie chicken than he probably ever imagined (and rarely complained). He jokes that rotisserie chicken should have been in our wedding vows.

And I must thank all my friends who helped edit this book; their eyes, their skills and their support means so much. So for everyone who helped me get to this moment, thank you, thank you, thank you. I deeply appreciate it.

Contents

Appetizers.................................... 9

Salads...................................... 25

Soups....................................... 39

Sandwiches 57

Main Courses 77

Desserts 111

Index 124

Appetizers

Garden Vegetable, Dill, Chicken Flatbread

Makes 2 flatbreads

This flatbread is so refreshing and perfect for summer. The sauce is a mixture of sour cream, dill, garlic and green onion that needs two hours to marinate, so prepare the sauce ahead of time.

This flatbread is made on a precooked naan crust which is soft and chewy (bake according to directions).

This recipe is perfect for a party because all the prep can be done in advance and you just assemble it at the last minute. It's also an inexpensive appetizer. I recommend buying the tomatoes and cucumbers from a local farmer because local produce tastes better and fresh is key to this flatbread.

1 ¼ cups sour cream

1 teaspoon dried dill weed

1 garlic clove, finely minced

1 green onion, chopped

1 (8.8 ounce) package of Stonefire Tandoori Baked Original Naan

½ cup chopped rotisserie chicken breasts

⅔ cup chopped cucumber

⅔ cup sliced grape or cherry tomatoes

1 teaspoon fresh lemon juice

1 teaspoon extra virgin olive oil

Salt and pepper

5 large fresh basil leaves to garnish

Mix sour cream, dill, chopped garlic and sliced green onion. Cover and refrigerate for 2 hours.

Cook your naan according to package directions.

When time to assemble, toss together chicken, cucumber, tomatoes, lemon juice and olive oil. Add salt to vegetables and toss.

Then spread half the sour cream mixture on flatbread crust. Top it with half the vegetable and chicken mixture. Finely slice the basil and sprinkle it on top. Repeat the process for the second flatbread, then slice and serve.

Enchilada Dip

Serves 6

This layered dip is so simple and delicious. I layer cream cheese, top it with cumin, then add refried beans, rotisserie chicken that has been tossed in enchilada sauce, and cover it with lots of cheese. Once it has been baked, it transforms into gooey goodness that is scooped up with tortilla chips. It's fantastic.

You can use red or green enchilada sauce, just be sure you use a sauce you like because it will heavily flavor the dip. If you don't like cilantro, you can garnish this with chopped avocado, or buy premade guacamole and pile that in the center. You can also add shredded iceberg lettuce in the middle. Leftovers are good warmed in the microwave (but don't reheat the entire dip, just scoop out what you need).

8 ounces cream cheese, softened

1 teaspoon ground cumin (you can substitute cumin seed for stronger cumin flavor)

1 ½ cups refried beans

2 ⅓ cups rotisserie chicken

10 ounces red or green enchilada sauce

½ cup drained corn

2 cups Mexican-style shredded cheese (or Taco style cheese)

Cilantro to garnish (optional)

Tortilla chips for serving

Guacamole to garnish (optional)

Set cream cheese on the counter for 30 minutes to soften it and make it easier to spread. If you forget that step, it will still spread, but it's a little harder.

While cream cheese softens, pull both breasts off the chicken and shred breast and a little thigh meat. Do not use any skin. Chop chicken, place in a bowl and cover with enchilada sauce and set aside. Drain corn and set aside. Preheat oven to 400 degrees.

If you plan to garnish with cilantro, cut off the stems and chop cilantro leaves. I like to use about half a cup and pile it in the center, that way anyone who doesn't like it can avoid it. If you know everyone likes it, or don't care, then chop as much as you want.

Spread cream cheese into bottom of a deep dish pie pan and sprinkle cumin over top.

Spread refried beans over that layer. Spread corn over the beans. Then spread chicken over that layer and top it with all the enchilada sauce. Top with shredded cheese and bake for 22-25 minutes. When done, garnish with cilantro and serve with tortilla chips. If desired, serve with guacamole.

Chilled Hot Wing Flatbread

Serves 2

This cool flatbread takes all the best parts of hot wings- like the sauce, celery and ranch dressing - and leaves behind the worst parts - like the fatty skin and fried chicken.

I toss baked rotisserie chicken breast in my favorite wing sauce, spread ranch on a chewy crust, add the chicken, and top it all with chopped celery and Gorgonzola crumbles. It's so easy and delicious. Wings make me feel sick after I eat a few, but I could eat this flatbread all day. If you've never tried it, Ott's makes a fantastic wing sauce that is not too spicy but incredibly flavorful and it's made in Missouri.

1 (8.8 ounce) package of Stonefire Tandoori Baked Original Naan

⅓ cup ranch dressing

⅔ cup chopped rotisserie chicken

2 -3 tablespoons Ott's Wing Sauce or your favorite hot wing sauce

2 small stalks of celery, minced

3 tablespoons crumbled Gorgonzola cheese

Cook flatbread according to package directions and set aside.

I recommend using the breast meat for this recipe. Pull off the chicken breast and finely chop it. Then toss it in the wing sauce and stir to coat the chicken.

Mince two small celery stalks.

Next, spread ranch dressing on a precooked flatbread. Top with the chicken. Sprinkle with celery and Gorgonzola and serve.

Southwest Egg Rolls

Serves 8 or more

This is one of my all-time favorite indulgent recipes. It takes me back to my college days when I'd order these at a restaurant, sip on a margarita and be in heaven. This is my take on a restaurant favorite and these are just as good. Your guests or family will be impressed when you serve these delightful bites.

½ cup canned corn, drained

½ cup black beans, drained

½ cup plus 2 tablespoons chunky salsa (a chunky salsa is a MUST)

1 tablespoon mayonnaise

½ cup Campbell's Fiesta Nacho Cheese Soup

2 cups diced rotisserie chicken, skin removed

¾ teaspoon cumin seed

3 tablespoons chives

1 tablespoon chopped cilantro

Egg roll wrappers

Canola or peanut oil

½ cup ranch dressing

½ cup chunky salsa

Thoroughly stir together the first nine ingredients. Note, that I say a chunky salsa is a must because you don't want too much liquid in the mixture.

Fill the egg rolls, following the directions on the back of the egg roll wrapper package on how to roll the egg rolls.

Only make about 10 and then start heating the oil. You can make the rest while the oil heats. Loosely cover the rolls with a slightly damp paper towel while you finish rolling them out.

Add oil to a large frying pan and heat over medium heat. You want about an inch of oil. Do not heat the oil too fast or it will brown the egg rolls too quickly.

When the egg rolls are all assembled, test the oil by dipping an edge of an egg roll in the oil. If it bubbles around the egg roll, then the oil is ready. Add egg rolls and fry 2-3 minutes per side or until golden brown. Drain on paper towels. Serve with dipping sauce.

For the dipping sauce, mix together the ranch and salsa and serve.

Chicken, Bacon Pizza with Sundried Tomatoes

Serves 4 as appetizer; 2 as main course

The sundried tomatoes and fresh basil really lift the flavor of this pizza; and of course, the bacon adds a lot, too. This pizza is easy, great for a quick dinner or a party.

1 ready-made pizza dough (Stonefire is my favorite brand)

Pizza sauce, desired amount

1 cup chopped, skinless rotisserie chicken

⅓ cup real bacon pieces (store bought is what I used)

¼ cup chopped sundried tomatoes

1 ⅓ cups shredded mozzarella cheese (or desired amount)

¼ cup feta cheese

Fresh basil to garnish

Preheat oven to 400 degrees.

Spread pizza sauce over dough. Top with chicken, bacon, sundried tomatoes and cheeses.

Bake for 15 to 18 minutes. Remove and garnish with slices of fresh basil. Allow to rest for 5 minutes before slicing.

Mediterranean Quesadillas with Feta, Red Pepper Sauce

Serves 3

I had a quesadilla party one night and offered a variety of quesadillas. This was one of the crowd's favorites. It's completely different than a traditional quesadilla and takes on Mediterranean flavors like hummus, cumin and olives. I top it with a delicious feta and roasted red pepper sauce.

This quesadilla is super easy to make so it's great for a busy weeknight or a party.

You can double the sauce recipe and serve it as a dip with pita chips (you don't even need the quesadillas, just serve this as a dip). It's one of my favorite party dips because it takes minutes to make and can be made a day in advance. It's always a huge hit.

Tip: You can buy jarred red bell peppers in most grocery stores for $2.50-$3 a jar, but many dollar stores sell them for $1. I always stock up when I am at a dollar store.

1 cup chopped, skinless rotisserie chicken

⅓ cup hummus, plus 1 tablespoon

1 tablespoon chopped red onion

½ teaspoon ground cumin

1 tablespoon chopped black olives

1 tablespoon chopped green olives

3 (8-inch) flour tortillas

¾ cup shredded mozzarella cheese

Sauce:

⅓ cup feta cheese

¾ cup jarred roasted red pepper slices

Make the sauce first. Place feta and roasted red pepper slices in a food processor and process for 30 seconds. Set aside.

Next, mix chicken, hummus, onion, cumin, and olives together and set aside.

Place mixture in half a flour tortilla shell (so when you fold it over it looks like a half moon). Top the mixture with cheese.

Preheat a nonstick skillet sprayed with cooking spray over medium heat. When hot, place the folded quesadilla down and cook about 3 minutes per side. Remove and top with red pepper sauce and serve immediately.

Chicken Mole Bites

Serves 8

When I started this recipe, I wanted to make chicken empanadas, but those are deep fried, unhealthy and time consuming to fill each one individually. I adore puff pastry because it's buttery, delicious and easy to work with. So I decided to fill puff pastry with this mole filling and bake it. It's sensational.

Note: You must defrost the puff pastry for this dish, so read the box for directions. There's a quick method and overnight method. If you don't defrost it properly, the puff pastry will tear as you try to use it.

2 Pepperidge Farm Puff Pastry sheets (1 box in the freezer section)

2 ½ cups chopped rotisserie chicken breast

⅓ cup sour cream

*⅔ to ¾ cup store-bought mole sauce (or to taste)

⅓ cup drained canned corn

⅓ cup chopped cilantro

*½ cup queso fresco (can substitute chevre or mozzarella balls if you don't find it)

1 cup shredded Mexican-cheese blend

Parchment paper

*Mole sauce is available in the Hispanic section of the grocery store. The strength will vary by brand, which is why I said to add it to taste. If you find you've added a little too much mole, you can mellow it out with more sour cream.

*Queso fresco just means fresh cheese in Spanish and it's available at Walmart, usually by the cheeses. It looks like mozzarella. I like to substitute chevre because it has a tangy finish, but a lot of people don't like goat cheese so if you're serving a crowd, I'd go with a milder cheese.

Defrost puff pastry according to package directions. Preheat oven to 400 degrees.

In a large bowl, mix together chicken, sour cream, mole sauce, corn, cilantro, and queso fresco.

Unroll one sheet of puff pastry. Place parchment paper on a large baking sheet and place puff pastry on one side of the pan. Fill it with half the chicken mixture and then sprinkle half the Mexican-cheese blend on top. Fold each side over to close it. Wet your fingers to seal the edges so the mixture doesn't bubble out as it cooks. Repeat with the other puff pastry.

Bake 18-22 minutes, until pastry turns golden and puffs up. Remove and allow to cool for 5-10 minutes before slicing.

Buffalo Chicken Pizza

Serves 3-4

My Buffalo Chicken Pizza is the perfect blend of spicy sauce, bubbling cheese, chewy pizza dough and heavenly cream cheese. I use cream cheese as the base and then top it with a chopped chicken breast, tossed in wing sauce and cheese.

I am a big believer that cream cheese makes the world better.

With only five ingredients, this is easy and scrumptious. My teenage nephew makes it every week.

The key is to use Ott's hot sauce, it has amazing flavor and a perfect balance of heat for most people (and it's made in Missouri). If you can't find Ott's, then use your favorite wing sauce. I try to make this spicy, but not unbearable because people like all different heat levels. If you have a party, you never know what people like.

This is great during football season. I will eat this over wings any day; I think you will too once you try this.

1 ready-made Stonefire pizza crust (can substitute 2 naans if you can't find the pizza crust or another pizza crust)

1 ⅓ cups chopped skinless rotisserie chicken breast only

½ cup Ott's hot sauce, plus more for drizzling

8 ounces of cream cheese, at room temperature

1 cup shredded mozzarella cheese

Preheat oven to 400 degrees. Toss chicken with hot sauce, stir to coat and set aside.

Spread cream cheese evenly over your pizza crust. When covered, spread chicken out across the pizza.

Top with cheese and then a slight drizzle of more hot sauce.

Bake 15-20 minutes until the cheese is melted to your desired consistency. Allow to cool for 5 minutes before slicing.

Creamy Gumbo Dip

Serves 6

This dip is incredible and perfect for any cold weather party like a Christmas soiree or Super Bowl gathering. It's unique which makes it stand out at an event where there's a lot of good dip competition.

My inspiration for this was gumbo and artichoke dip. From gumbo, I took the chicken, andouille sausage and "trinity" (bell peppers, celery and onion) and then mixed that with gooey cheese and heavenly cream cheese found in so many artichoke dips. I use Cajun seasoning, but be sure to taste the seasoning before you add it to this dip because so many brands are appallingly salty. I use "Joe's Stuff" which I discovered at the New Orleans School of Cooking. We order it online: http://www.neworleansschoolofcooking.com Use Cajun seasoning sparingly or you could ruin this.

Tip: This dip can be assembled a day in advance, refrigerated overnight and baked right before the party. Be sure to let it rest on the counter for 15 minutes before you bake it.

¾ cup minced andouille sausage

1 teaspoon canola oil

1 large stalk of celery, chopped

½ cup chopped red onion

¼ cup chopped red bell pepper

¼ cup chopped green bell pepper

⅛ teaspoon salt

4 ounces cream cheese

¼ teaspoon Cajun seasoning

⅔ cup mayonnaise

¾ cup chopped, skinless rotisserie chicken breast

1 ⅓ cups shredded Monterey Jack-Cheddar blend

Preheat oven to 400 degrees. Chop all ingredients and set aside.

Heat a large frying pan over medium heat. When hot, add andouille sausage and oil. Then add celery and onion and cook for 3 minutes. Add bell peppers and salt and cook another 2 minutes. Remove from heat and immediately stir in cream cheese and Cajun seasoning. Then stir in mayonnaise, chicken and half the cheese. Spread mixture into a deep dish pie pan and cover with remaining cheese.

Bake 15-20 minutes until it bubbles on top. Serve with tortilla chips or French bread slices. It's amazing!

Salads

It doesn't happen very often, but there are nights when I am so exhausted I can't fathom turning on the stove. That's when the rotisserie chicken comes to the rescue and I usually whip up a salad.

If you keep bagged salads on hand - like Caesar - you can top it with rotisserie chicken, serve a nice roll and you have dinner.

I love to add sliced chicken to a bag of Asian slaw and boil edamame and toss it all together.

Another easy idea is I take a bag of arugula, top it with blueberries, sliced strawberries, red onion, chopped chicken, walnuts or sunflower seeds, goat cheese and toss it with a raspberry vinaigrette.

Whenever you have a recipe that requires you to chop salad vegetables like cucumbers, lettuce, bell peppers, just chop extra and put it aside for tomorrow. It's best to store the vegetables in separate containers or baggies.

Although it's more expensive, sometimes it's worth buying items like shredded carrots that you can toss in your salad to save yourself time.

I boil a bag of shelled edamame every week and keep it refrigerated and then sprinkle those to my salad.

Whenever I make rotini pasta, I make a little extra to serve on a lunch salad the next day; that adds bulk and carbs to my salad. I toss chopped chicken, edamame, pasta and other vegetables with lettuce and have a salad hearty enough to hold me over for dinner.

To keep it interesting, I try to theme my salads. For example, I will do a Mediterranean and use feta cheese, cucumber, dill, tomato, chicken and toss it in a homemade lemon and olive oil vinaigrette. Or, as you'll see in my "Ode to Wine Country" salad, I use components from one region (like wine country).

Dried fruit, sunflower seeds and nuts are staples in my house and are a quick addition to salad.

Fresh herbs really liven up a salad and are healthy. My favorite additions are basil, parsley, dill and cilantro. Dried dill adds wonderful flavor, too.

One thing to note about this chapter is I have several chicken salad recipes. I have split my chicken salads between my Sandwiches and Salads chapters because some of the recipes are better on lettuce and some are tastier on bread. There's an excellent variety of both.

I hope you enjoy them.

Southwest Quinoa Salad with Cumin-Lime Dressing

Makes 4 servings

This is now my favorite summer dish. I am so in love with this quinoa salad. It's healthy, refreshing, low fat, high in fiber, high in protein and loaded with vitamins. And, did I mention it's delicious?

First, I cook the quinoa with chicken broth (or stock) to give it more flavor. Then, I chill it and toss it with chicken, cilantro, red bell peppers, corn, avocado and a lime-cumin vinaigrette. Sliced grape tomatoes are a nice addition.

Note: The quinoa should be made in advance and chilled before you add the rest of the ingredients, for best results.

This is perfect for lunch as a main course; as a side dish at a picnic; or as a light dinner.

Tip: Whenever I work with avocadoes, I always buy at least one extra because it's not uncommon to open one and find black spots and have to toss part of it.

1 cup uncooked quinoa

2 cups low-sodium chicken broth

2 cups chopped rotisserie chicken (breast is preferred in this recipe)

Half a large red bell pepper

1 ½ tablespoons red onion

½ cup of chopped cilantro

1 cup of canned corn, drained

½ cup black beans, drained

2 avocadoes

Dressing:

3 tablespoons fresh lime juice

1 tablespoon, plus 1 teaspoon canola oil

2 teaspoons honey

1 teaspoon ground cumin

For the quinoa: Bring quinoa and chicken broth to a boil in a medium pot with a tight-fitting lid. Let it boil 3 minutes, reduce heat to medium-low, cover with lid and cook another 15 minutes. Quinoa is done when a hook is released from the grain. Chill for later.

To prepare: Chop chicken, red bell pepper, onion and cilantro and place in a medium to large bowl. Fluff the quinoa and add it to the mix.

Drain corn and black beans and toss with quinoa. Then pit your avocado and chop it into small chunks.

Whisk the dressing ingredients together and pour over quinoa. Toss to coat, and serve.

If you are making this ahead of time, leave the avocado off until the last minute.

Note: This recipe is also good with about ½ cup halved grape tomatoes, too.

Ode to Wine Country

Serves 2

I call this "Ode to Wine Country" because it's a beautiful salad of arugula and spinach, figs poached in Moscato, globe grapes, walnuts, chicken and a Moscato dressing with a hint of rosemary. These are the some of the flavors found in wine country.

This salad comes together in about 10 minutes but tastes like a salad you'd get in an upscale restaurant. It is healthy and practically effortless.

Tip: If you don't regularly drink Moscato, buy one of the airplane-size bottles for the recipe.

⅔ cup inexpensive Moscato (you're using it to poach, so it doesn't need to be an expensive bottle)

6 dried figs

4 cups mixed arugula and spinach mix (you can also substitute a spring mix of greens)

12 globe grapes

12 walnut halves

1 ½ tablespoons minced red onion

⅔ cup chopped rotisserie chicken

2 teaspoon extra virgin olive oil

2 teaspoon balsamic vinegar

6 teaspoons Moscato liquid reserved from poaching

¼ teaspoon dried rosemary, crumbled

¼ teaspoon honey

Goat cheese crumbles (optional)

Place Moscato in a small pot and turn the heat on to medium. While it heats, slice figs in half and set aside.

Next, divide the greens between two plates. Rinse the grapes off and slice in half. Divide the grapes and walnuts evenly between the plates. Next, chop the onion and chicken and divide that between the plates.

By now, your Moscato should be bubbling. Add the figs and poach for 3 minutes. Remove figs immediately, but reserve the Moscato liquid.

In a bowl, whisk together the olive oil, balsamic vinegar, 6 tablespoons of the Moscato liquid, rosemary and honey. Pour over salad and toss thoroughly. If desired, add goat cheese.

Add salt and pepper to taste and serve.

Chicken, Corn, Avocado and Black Bean Salad in Chipotle Dressing

Serves 2

1 head of Romaine lettuce

1 ear of corn

1 ¼ cups chopped rotisserie chicken breast

⅓ cup black beans, drained

1 avocado

2 Campari tomatoes

⅓ cup mayonnaise

¼ cup Pace Southwest Chipotle Salsa

1 tablespoon fresh lime juice

Tortilla chips

Shredded cheese to garnish

Cilantro to garnish (optional)

Place corn in its husk in the microwave and cook for 3 ½ minutes. Remove and when it's cool enough to handle, shuck it and slice corn off the cob. Set aside.

Tear Romaine into pieces and divide between two bowls.

Pull chicken breast off the chicken and discard skin. Chop and sprinkle over salad.

Drain your black beans and divide between the salads.

Slice avocado in half and cut each half into slices and place half an avocado on each salad.

Chop tomatoes and divide between the salads. Sprinkle corn over salads.

For the dressing, whisk together mayonnaise, salsa and lime juice. Drizzle over salads. Garnish each plate or bowl with tortilla chips. Sprinkle with cheese and garnish with fresh cilantro.

Ultimate Classic Chicken Salad

Everyone has their favorite classic chicken salad recipe and this is mine. It combines tender chicken, crunchy pecans, tart cranberries, sweet white grapes and the fresh taste of celery. I think this is a winner.

3 ½ cups chopped rotisserie chicken

½ cup coarsely chopped pecans

2 tablespoons dried cranberries

½ cup chopped celery

½ cup halved white grapes

⅓ cup chopped red onion

¾ cup mayonnaise

2 teaspoons white wine vinegar (can substitute apple cider vinegar)

1 teaspoon sugar

Salt and pepper to taste

Remove skin from the rotisserie chicken and pull the meat off the bones. You will use most of the chicken for this recipe, but not all. Chop chicken into chunks.

In a large bowl, add the first six ingredients (through the red onion) and toss gently.

In another bowl, whisk together mayonnaise, vinegar and sugar. Stir together until chicken salad is well coated. Add salt and pepper to taste. Serve or cover and refrigerate until it's time to serve.

Asian Chicken Salad

Serves 4

This is one of my favorite chicken salad recipes. When I started creating these recipes, my husband said "You're not going to make chicken salad, are you? Everyone does that."

Well, everyone does it because just about everyone loves it. So now I have whipped up about 10 varieties, but this is one of the most unique and delicious.

I have served this on Ritz crackers at parties and it was a huge hit. I have piled it in the middle of a salad and devoured it for lunch (it's so moist, no extra dressing is needed). And I have served it on French bread as a sandwich and that's pretty fantastic, too. I recommend topping the sandwich with thinly sliced cucumbers.

They key to this salad is you must have Soy Vay Veri Veri Teriyaki sauce. If you've never used that sauce, you should. It's one of my favorite kitchen condiments.

Tip: Leftover Soy Vay Veri Veri Teriyaki sauce can be used as a sauce for stir-fry, to flavor soba noodles, or as a marinade (leave sliced beef or pork in this sauce overnight in the fridge and grill it the next day). It's so versatile. You can search stores in your area on the website to see if they carry it or order it online: https://www.soyvay.com

3 ½ cups chopped rotisserie chicken, skin removed

¾ cup mayonnaise

⅓ cup Soy Vay Veri Veri Teriyaki sauce

2 stalks of celery, minced

3 green onions, sliced

⅓ shredded carrot

¼ cup chopped cilantro

Pepper to taste (you don't need salt)

1 cucumber, sliced

Bed of iceberg lettuce

While I am not an iceberg lettuce fan, if you are serving this on lettuce, iceberg is the way to go. It's so crisp and light and is a beautiful complement to the salad.

First, assemble the chicken salad part of the meal.

In a large bowl, mix mayonnaise and Soy Vay sauce together. Then add chicken, celery, onion, carrots and cilantro. Stir until thoroughly combined. Add pepper to taste and serve.

Serve it over lettuce with cucumbers.

Like any chicken salad, this gets better with time, but of all the chicken salad recipes, this is the most flavorful without having time to marinate.

Barbecue Ranch Chicken Salad

Serves 2 as a main; 4 as a side salad

This restaurant quality salad is amazing and was inspired by my favorite salad at The Cheesecake Factory. This is not quite as good, but it is pretty close. Salads don't often "wow" people, but this one usually does. My brother-in-law calls is the "the bomb." It pleases even non-salad eaters.

1 head of romaine lettuce

⅔ cup of canned corn, drained

⅔ cup black beans, drained

1 ¼ cups chopped chicken

2 Roma tomatoes, chopped

3 slices of bacon or ⅓ cup real bacon pieces

½ cup shredded cheddar cheese

French's Fried Onion rings (like you use for the green bean casserole at Thanksgiving)

Dressing:

½ cup Ranch dressing

1 ½ tablespoons barbecue sauce

1 tablespoon salsa

Get a large serving bowl for this recipe. For the photo, I made this look pretty by stacking the ingredients, but you will need to toss this together with the dressing before you serve it.

Chop lettuce and place in a bowl. Add corn, black beans, chicken, tomatoes, bacon and cheese.

Mix ingredients for the dressing together then pour dressing over salad and thoroughly toss to distribute ingredients and the dressing. Allow to rest for 5 minutes and then serve.

Hawaiian Chicken Salad

Serves 4

I've been playing around with this concept of a Hawaiian chicken salad for quite some time, and I have not been happy with the results -- until now.

I initially made this with macadamia nuts, but they didn't offer enough crunch. So I decided on cashews, but I am allergic to cashews.

No worries, I thought, I will be sure not to touch the nuts, and I'll be fine. Wrong. As I stirred this salad (I was taking it to a ladies gathering that night), I started to turn bright red! I got hives down my neck and throat and started to consider a trip to urgent care. Luckily, it only lasted about 30 minutes.

But now I know not only am I allergic to cashews, I am highly allergic. To make a long story short, I survived and the chicken salad was a big hit. I am sure it will be your party, too. I won't be making it again.

1 rotisserie chicken	*¾ cup cashews*
½ cup chopped red onion	*¾ cup mayonnaise*
1 cup minced fresh pineapple	*1 teaspoon red wine vinegar*
⅓ cup chopped celery	*¼ teaspoon sugar*
12 basil leaves	*Salt and pepper to taste*

Bed of mixed spring greens or tortilla chips to serve

Remove all the skin from the rotisserie chicken and discard. Then, pull the meat off the bones and chop the entire chicken into pieces. Place it in a large container with a lid.

Chop onion, pineapple and celery, and thinly slice the basil leaves. Add to the bowl. Top with cashews.

Stir together mayonnaise, red wine vinegar and sugar. Add to the dish and stir to coat. Add salt and pepper to taste. For best results, cover and refrigerate 2 hours before serving.

You can serve this as a salad on a bed of mixed greens, but it's also wonderful as an appetizer served with tortilla chips or crackers.

Soups

Slow Cooker Stock

Makes 7-8 cups

I've experimented a lot with slow cooker stock. My first batch tasted like watered down stock. The next was a little better, but still not rich enough.

I make a ton of traditional stock, but the problem with a slow cooker is it doesn't maintain that simmer all day, like the stove does, to extract the flavor needed. So I realized I needed to add a punch of flavor in the ingredients. After many attempts, I have finally come up with this recipe that uses two chicken carcasses, parsley, dried mushrooms (which are key) and a hint of soy sauce. The result is a beautiful, dark, rich stock.

This will yield 7-8 cups of stock, so you probably want to freeze any extra.

If you are single and don't want to buy two chickens at a time, just freeze a carcass when you're done with one and the next time you buy one, make this stock.

When making this, it's important that you use the chicken skin, too. I never eat the skin because it's so unhealthy, but it's loaded with fat and it is well seasoned, which adds flavor to your stock.

I also love how easy this is. I don't have to monitor it like I do a stovetop stock. I toss it in and forget about it.

If you have to go buy all these ingredients, then this will be more expensive than store-bought stock, and not really worth it. But I always have all these ingredients on hand, so I make home-made stock all the time. I prefer the flavor and it has less sodium than commercial brands. If you are watching your sodium level, skip the soy sauce in this recipe. Plus, I freeze it so I can grab stock whenever I need.

The difference between a stock and broth, is the stock is produced by cooking down the bones and other connective tissues; whereas a broth just has to have meat in the cooking process. A stock is more flavorful and is usually preferred. You can substitute homemade stock for any recipe that calls for broth.

Tip: I use stock for so many dishes, not just soup. It's an excellent way to flavor rice, couscous, risotto, pasta, and sauces. I poach frozen tilapia in equal parts stock and white wine. I sprinkle the fish with a heavy dose of dill weed and a squeeze of lemon at the end. Dinner is ready in about 10 minutes and the fish is healthy and flavored from the wine and stock. It's a quick and inexpensive dinner.

8 cups water

2 rotisserie chicken carcasses (it's nice if there's a little meat left on the bones)

1 teaspoon peppercorns

3 bay leaves

2 large carrots, ends chopped off

1 large yellow onion, peeled and sliced into chunks

4 stalks of celery with the leaves, rinsed to remove dirt

1 clove chopped garlic or 1 teaspoon dehydrated garlic

⅓ cup dried porcini mushrooms or another dried mushroom, like shiitake

½ teaspoon soy sauce

¼ cup fresh parsley with stems

Place all ingredients in a large slow cooker. Cover and cook on high for 6-8 hours. Note, if you have a slow cooker that cooks in hours instead of heat- for example 4 hours, 6 hours, 10 hours— then if possible, cook it on 4 hours and then when it's done, hit 4 hours again. This will be the highest possible temperature, which will yield the best results.

Traditional Stock

Makes 4-5 cups

10 cups cold water

1 rotisserie chicken carcass (it's nice if there's a little meat left on the bones)

¼ teaspoon peppercorns

2 bay leaves

2 carrots, coarsely chopped

1 large yellow onion, sliced into chunks

2 stalks of celery with the leaves, rinsed

Handful of fresh parsley with stems

½ teaspoon salt

Place all ingredients in a large stock pot and bring to a boil (you want the ingredients to be submerged in water). Then reduce to a simmer for 4 hours. Keep an eye on the pot, you may need to add 1 cup of water at a time to make sure the bones and vegetables stay covered.

After 4 hours turn off the heat and allow it to cool slightly, then strain. Stock is ready to be used.

Tip: This stock is great for making traditional chicken noodle soup. I bring it to a boil, add 1 cup of frozen carrots and peas, rotini noodles and ½ teaspoon thyme leaves. Boil until pasta is tender and add in a desired amount of chicken to heat through. You can also use day-old rice instead of noodles, but instead of adding the rice with the vegetables, cook until the vegetables are tender and then add the rice and chicken and heat through.

Asian Stock

Makes 4-5 cups

10 cups cold water

1 rotisserie chicken carcass (it's nice if there's a little meat left on the bones)

¼ teaspoon peppercorns

2 carrots

1 large yellow onion

½ -inch piece of ginger

2 stalks of celery with the leaves

½ cup dried shiitake mushrooms

1 teaspoon soy sauce

Place all ingredients in a large stock pot and bring to a boil. Reduce to a slow simmer for 4-5 hours. Skim any scum off the top that may form. Keep an eye on the pot, you may need to add 1 cup of water at a time as the stock boils down. You want to make sure the ingredients are covered with water at all times.

When ready, turn off the heat and allow it to cool slightly, then strain. Stock is ready to be used.

Tip: This stock makes a nice egg drop soup, which is so easy. First, boil 2/3 cup of sliced, dried shiitake mushrooms for 7 minutes in the stock. Then whisk together 3 large eggs in a bowl and then drizzle it into the stock. Add 2 cups of chopped chicken (that's not traditional but I like the protein) and 3 sliced green onions and heat through. You will probably want to add some soy sauce or sesame oil to taste before serving.

Chicken and Dumpling Soup

Serves 4-5

This soup is incredibly comforting. I wish I could take credit for using the tortillas to make dumplings, but I cannot. A former friend's aunt made a version of this soup and she introduced me to the idea. I usually hate chicken and dumpling soup because it's often bland, but this soup is wonderful. So if you don't traditionally like dumpling soup, I encourage you to try this.

This delicious, creamy soup comes together quickly and your family will gobble it up just as fast.

1 tablespoon canola oil

1 medium onion

2 stalks celery

1 (15-ounce) can chicken broth

1 (10-ounce) can cream of chicken soup

1 soup can filled with water

1 ⅓ cups mixed frozen peas and carrots

2 cups chopped rotisserie chicken

3 (6-inch) flour tortillas

Chop onion and celery and set aside.

Place tortillas on top of each other and use a knife or pizza cutter to cut into ½-inch rectangles or squares. Set aside.

Heat oil in a medium-large pot over medium heat. When hot, add onions and celery and cook for 5 minutes. Add chicken stock, cream of chicken soup and then fill the soup can with water and add to the pot. Toss in frozen peas and carrots and bring to a boil for 3 minutes, stirring constantly. Reduce to strong simmer and add chicken and tortillas. The tortillas serve as dumplings. Cook 8-10 minutes. Add salt and pepper to taste and serve.

Light Chicken and Corn Chowder

Serves 4

2 tablespoons canola oil

1 large yellow onion

3 stalks celery

1 heaping tablespoon flour

1 large Russet potato

¼ teaspoon salt

2 cups chicken stock (homemade is best)

1 bay leaf

2 cups whole milk

1 (15-ounce) can creamed corn

1 (15-ounce) can corn

2 cups chopped rotisserie chicken breast

Salt and pepper to taste

Chop onion, celery, potato and set aside. I don't peel the potato.

Heat 2 tablespoons of oil in large pot over medium heat. When hot, add onions and celery and cook 2 minutes. Then add flour and cook 5 minutes. Add potato, salt, stock and bay leaf and bring to a boil for 5 minutes. Reduce heat to strong simmer and add milk and corn and cook about 12 minutes or until potatoes are just tender. Add chicken at the last minute just to heat through.

The vegetables should still be slightly crunchy. This lighter version of chowder uses milk instead of half and half or cream but it's still packed with flavor. It's an excellent soup and easy to make.

Vegetable, Barley and Chicken Soup

Serves 5

I love this soup because it's packed with vegetables and feels nourishing. My 3-year-old gobbles this up.

This soup has a lot of ingredients, but don't let that deter you from trying it. It's a simple soup that is on the table in 30 minutes and it's healthy so you can feel good about feeding it to your family.   The barley adds fiber and helps thicken the soup. It's important to use a quick cooking variety of barley because it only cooks 15 minutes before you serve it and regular barley takes longer to soften.

Leftovers keep for several days and it freezes well, too.

The chicken goes in at the very end, so to save yourself prep time, chop the chicken while the soup is boiling.

Tip: There are a couple ways you can shave a little prep time off. Buy a bag of coleslaw mix instead of chopping your cabbage; buy precut mushrooms; precut carrots; and use dehydrated garlic instead of fresh.

1 large yellow onion	*1 zucchini*
2 carrots	*2 bay leaves*
1 ½ cups chopped white cabbage	*1 garlic clove, chopped*
2 stalks celery	*Salt and pepper to taste*
1 tablespoon canola oil	*7 cups chicken stock*
1 teaspoon Italian seasoning	*⅔ cup quick cooking barley*
¼ teaspoon dried rosemary	*2 ½ cups chopped, skinless rotisserie chicken*
1 pint sliced baby portabella mushrooms	

Chop onion, cabbage, carrots and celery and set aside. Cut zucchini into quarters horizontally, and then slice those pieces. Slice mushrooms and set aside.

In a large stock pot, heat oil over medium-high heat. When hot, add onion, cabbage, carrots and celery and cook 5 minutes, stirring occasionally. Then add Italian seasoning and rosemary, mushrooms, zucchini, salt and pepper and cook another 3 minutes. Add bay leaves, garlic, stock and barley and bring to a boil. Reduce heat to medium and cook 12-15 minutes. While the soup cooks, chop your chicken. Drop in chopped chicken and heat through before serving.

Chicken Pho

Serves 2-3

This is a wonderful, rich soup. It's easy, satisfying and healthy. I love it. The mushrooms in the broth give it a dark, rich color and flavor.

The key is to thinly slice the carrots. You can substitute thinly sliced cabbage, bok choy or even coleslaw mix for a quick soup.

Tip: Make the stock and noodles on Sunday and then finish off the soup on Monday. With that advance prep, it will be ready in 15 minutes.

4 cups of my Asian Chicken stock

Handful of dehydrated mushrooms, such as morels or shiitake

1 thinly sliced carrot

¼ cup thinly sliced red onion

2 handfuls sugar snap peas (split in half)

6 slices of dehydrated garlic

4 ounces of cooked and drained Soba noodles

2 handfuls of fresh spinach

2 rotisserie chicken breasts, sliced

Sesame oil

Cilantro to garnish

Bean sprouts (optional)

Make Soba noodles according to package directions. Drizzle with sesame oil and set aside (these can be made a day ahead and kept in the refrigerator).
Bring your stock to a boil and add mushrooms, onions, carrots, sugar snap peas and garlic. Cook for 7 minutes. Then add noodles, spinach and chicken just until heated through.

Plate the soup and add a few drops (just drops as sesame oil is strong) to each bowl. Serve garnished with fresh cilantro and if desired, bean sprouts.

White Chili

Serves 6

White chili seems to be one of those divisive soups: people love it or hate it. Some people feel like any chili that doesn't contain beef isn't really chili. I enjoy white chili because I love the pronounced flavors of cumin and sour cream and the tender chunks of chicken.

There are so many versions of this dish, but I add corn to mine. I like to top it with cheese or avocados. Tortilla chips are a good topping, too.

1 tablespoon canola oil

1 cup chopped yellow onion

2 teaspoons cumin seed

1 ½ teaspoons ground cumin powder

2 teaspoons chili powder

1 yellow bell pepper

1 (32 ounce) box of low sodium chicken broth, plus 2 cups of regular broth

1 cup water

1 teaspoon chopped garlic or dried garlic

1 cup half and half

¾ cup sour cream

1 (4-ounces) can chopped green chilies

¼ cup chopped cilantro

2 (15-ounce) cans cannellini beans

1 (15-ounce) can corn, drained

4 cups chopped rotisserie chicken

This has a lot of ingredients, but it's still an easy dish.

Chop onion, yellow bell pepper and chicken and set aside.

In a large pot, heat oil over medium heat. When hot, add onion, cumin seed, cumin and chili powder. Cook 5 minutes and then add yellow bell pepper and sauté another 3 minutes. Then add the next nine ingredients (everything but the chicken) and cook over medium to medium-low heat for 10 minutes. Once you add the sour cream, you don't want to let the soup boil because it could curdle, so keep the heat at medium.

Add chicken and cook 5 more minutes. Serve with tortilla chips or avocado or shredded cheese.

Quick Posole

Serves 4

If you have 15 minutes, then you can have dinner on the table. That's right, from start to finish, this soup will only take you 15 minutes.

Here's another piece of good news: this flavorful fare boasts only 220 calories a bowl.

Posole is a stew popular in Colombia and Mexico that is slow cooked and contains hominy. While it is traditionally slow cooked, I don't have time for that so I came up with this snappy version. It's actually inspired by a friend's slow cooker pork posole recipe.

It's flavored with broth (or stock), green enchilada sauce, cilantro, cumin, salsa and then a squeeze of lime. The shredded chicken is so tender in this dish.

I assume everyone has a food processor, but if you don't, then add a couple extra minutes to the cooking time (and then go buy yourself one). I have a cheap one that I paid $10 for in 2000. I am not kidding. So there's no need to save up for a good one; this has served me well. I always use it to chop onions. You only need to chop an onion and cilantro for this dish, so there's not a lot of chopping anyway.

1 teaspoon canola oil

1 yellow onion

1 bunch cilantro

½ teaspoon cumin seed

¾ teaspoon ground cumin

1 (15-ounce) can reduced sodium chicken broth or homemade stock

1 (10-ounce) can green enchilada sauce

2 cups water

1 (15-ounce) can yellow hominy

⅔ cup salsa (red or green will work; I prefer red)

2 cups skinless, shredded rotisserie chicken

1 lime for serving

Chop onion and cilantro set aside. When chopping cilantro, I just keep it as a bunch, chop the stems off where the leaves end and then chop that part, including stems. Some people take the time to pick off leaves, but not me. That takes forever. Stems are fine in the soup.

In a medium pot, heat oil and add onion and cumin and cook 5 minutes or until onion is tender. Add cilantro, broth, enchilada sauce, water, hominy, salsa and cook 5 minutes. While that cooks, shred your chicken and then add it to the pot and cook 5 more minutes.

Note: the easiest way to shred is pull off the skin, pull the chicken off the bone and shred it by hand. I always save the skin and bones for stock. You can freeze that if you won't have time to make it this week. I find two birds boiled together makes a better stock anyway.

Serve with a lime wedge. If you want add more vegetables, you can serve this with chopped avocado and tomatoes.

Chicken Tortilla Soup

Serves 4-5

From start to finish, this soup takes 25 minutes.

If you enjoy the flavors of cumin, cilantro and corn, you should love this. It's also a light choice: a bowl has roughly 310 calories.

It freezes well, so if you are single or travel a lot, you can easily freeze it into individual portions. This is one of my favorite soups.

1 teaspoon canola oil

1 large yellow onion

1 ½ teaspoons ground cumin

1 teaspoon chili powder

½ teaspoon cumin seed

1 large red bell pepper

*1 garlic clove or dash of dehydrated garlic

1 (32-ounce) box of reduced sodium chicken broth

1 (15-ounce) can of corn, drained

½ a bunch of cilantro

4 corn tortillas

1 tablespoon cornmeal (if you don't have any, just add 2 more tortillas)

1 ½ cups chunky salsa (your favorite brand)

Meat from 1 rotisserie chicken

Avocado to garnish (optional)

*If you want to save time and you're not cooking with dehydrated garlic, you need to buy some. It's awesome! I tried it when I visited the New Orleans School of Cooking and I was skeptical, but was instantly won over. Now I only use fresh garlic if I am making a dressing or something that must have it. Dehydrated garlic saves me time and effort – and I don't have stinky hands. You can order it online, but I recently bought some from Big Lots, of all places. It was inexpensive, too. I'd call your local store before heading over. It's sold in the spice section in a jar that looks like a spice jar.

First, chop onion and red bell pepper and set aside (use a food processor, if you have it).

Split a head of cilantro in half and cut the stems off one half. Then bunch up the leaves and slice those and set aside.

In a large pot, heat the oil over medium heat. When hot, add onion, cumin, chili powder and cumin seed. Stir occasionally while it cooks for about 7 minutes. While that cooks, do the next steps but be sure to stir the onion so it doesn't burn. *Continued on page 56*

Pile tortillas on top of each other, slice them and then cut into small squares and set aside.

Tear the meat off your chicken. Discard the skin or save it for another use. Coarsely chop the chicken and set aside (if you have time; if not, you will get to that in a second).

When onion is tender, add all the ingredients from the bell pepper through the salsa. You do not want to add the chicken yet because it's already cooked. Bring soup to a soft boil and cook 10 minutes.

Finish chopping your chicken, if you haven't already

When soup has cooked 10 minutes, drop chicken in and turn off the heat. The soup is piping hot and will quickly heat the meat.

Serve with a slice of avocado, crumbled up tortilla chips, cheese or plain.

Sandwiches

On a hectic weeknight, we've all succumbed to ordering pizza for dinner, but the next time you're tempted to do that, open this chapter. It's full of delicious, easy recipes that you can get on the table faster than you can order pizza.

The first important step in making a great sandwich is selecting the right bread. I switch it up and change between ciabatta, baguette, Italian bread, Hawaiian rolls, hoagies, regular sandwich bread, pita, pita pockets, tortillas and wraps.

And if you have leftover bread, use it in your next meal. When planning a weekly menu, I think about what will be left over from a recipe and work that ingredient in later in the week.

I freeze leftover baguettes and transform them into crostini when I am entertaining.

If I know I have a busy day ahead then I plan to make sandwiches with soup or salad for dinner. Serve it with a side of steamed vegetables and call it a day. And I try to plan ahead for the week, too. If I'm making soup on Monday, then I will plan to have sandwiches on Tuesday and pair it with leftover soup and make a salad.

This chapter is full of excellent sandwich recipes but I also have quick ideas that don't warrant a recipe because they are so easy. Here are a few:

Make a mock Monte Cristo Sandwich. Take a slice of chicken breast, a few slices of ham, slice of Gouda and place it all on a thick slice of bread. Spread raspberry jam on the interior of the sandwich, generously butter the outside and grill it like you would a grilled cheese sandwich. Sprinkle with powdered sugar before serving. Traditionally, Monte Cristos are fried, so this is a healthier choice. (10 minutes)

Create a jerk chicken sandwich by sprinkling chicken breast with jerk seasoning, then placing it on a bun with sliced mango, red onion, mayonnaise and cilantro. I buy jarred mango which makes this sandwich even easier. (10 minutes)

Make a chicken pot pie sandwich. Bake a batch of refrigerated buttermilk biscuits. Cut up about 3 cups of chicken and make a can of either Cream of Chicken or Cream of Mushroom Soup (your choice). While biscuits bake, drop the chicken in the soup with ½ cup of peas. When biscuits are ready, use a slotted spoon to remove chicken and peas from the soup and stuff into the warm biscuits which double as sandwich bread. (20 minutes)

A chicken Caesar wrap is another delicious choice and insanely easy. I make a bag of Caesar salad, chop up chicken and roll it in either a whole wheat wrap or a high protein wrap. (10 minutes) Those are some quick ideas. I hope you enjoy the rest of my sandwich recipes.

Curried Chicken Salad

Serves 4-5

I make amazing curried chicken salad. It has everything from dried cranberries to shredded coconut; it's wonderful.

It is good stuffed in pita pockets, scooped out on a pile of lettuce for a salad, stuffed in a whole wheat tortilla wrap or even served at a party as an appetizer in puff pastry cups or as a dip with tortilla chips. It's so versatile. When I serve it as a salad, I like to add chopped green apples on the side and sometimes red bell pepper.

Tip: You may have leftover pita from this recipe. Here's a way to use it for breakfast: stuff pita pockets with almond butter and sliced banana and dried dates. For a quick lunch, use pita as pizza dough and top with sauce, cheese and sliced vegetables. Bake at 400 for 8 minutes. Pita freezes well so that's an option, too, if you're not ready to use it this week.

1 rotisserie chicken

2/3 cup sliced green grapes

2 tablespoons chopped cilantro

1/3 cup chopped red onion

2 stalks celery

1/3 cup shredded sweetened coconut

1/2 cup dried cranberries

1 cup mayonnaise

1 cup Light Miracle Whip

1 1/2 teaspoons curry powder (or to taste)

Salt and pepper to taste

Whole wheat pita pockets to serve

De-skin and de-bone your chicken. I save the skin and bones for stock. You can freeze them for that if you don't plan to make stock any time soon. Then tear all the meat off the bird and chop it. I use everything, down to the wings.

Place chicken in a large bowl. Take about 20 grapes and slice them into thirds. Add the grapes to the chicken. Chop cilantro, red onion and celery and add it to the mix. Top with shredded coconut and dried cranberries.

In another bowl, mix mayonnaise and Light Miracle Whip. Stir in curry powder and add a little salt and pepper. I use 1 1/2 teaspoons but if you have a poor quality curry powder, you may need as much as a tablespoon. Taste as you go so you don't ruin it.

Then stir mayonnaise mixture into chicken and stir until thoroughly combined. Cover and refrigerate for 2 hours before serving to let the flavors marry.

Chicken and Andouille Po' Boy with Horseradish Slaw

Makes 6 sandwiches (people usually eat more than one)

This was one of my favorite inventions of 2014. I love Louisiana food. My husband is from there and we visit every year, but New Orleans has been one of my favorite food cities since long before we met.

Last summer, I wanted to invent an easy Po' boy, one of my favorite sandwiches. A lot of Po' boys are fried and I wanted something lighter, so I mixed lean chicken breast with spicy andouille (a Cajun sausage) and topped it with a spicy slaw. The horseradish slaw makes this dish. It's fantastic!

The slaw is best made two hours in advance to let the flavors marinate. If you don't have that amount of time, make one and a half times the slaw's dressing recipe so there's more sauce on it (but keep in mind the leftovers will be even spicier).

Andouille is a smoked pork Cajun sausage and it's traditionally spicy. If you don't like a lot of spice, you could use Johnsonville New Orleans style andouille, which is not very spicy; or even use kielbasa.

If you do like a little kick and you're in the Springfield, Missouri, area, try Circle B Ranch's andouille. Circle B Ranch is a heritage breed hog farm in Seymour, Missouri, where hogs are humanely raised. I've been there and the hogs graze freely. I like that. You can find the product at many stores in Missouri as well as the Greater Springfield Farmers Market. One bite and you can tell there are no fillers. But it is spicy, so keep that in mind if you're sensitive to heat because the slaw has a little kick. You can find more information about Circle B Ranch at www.circlebranchpork.com.

This recipe was featured on an episode of Ozarks Live with Joy Robertson and Tom Trtan and they loved it. *Continued on page 62*

Tip: You will have leftover horseradish slaw, so I often serve pulled pork or chicken the next day to use up the slaw. It's also fantastic on salmon patty sandwiches. For another easy dinner, pull the meat off a rotisserie chicken, toss it with your favorite barbecue sauce and then serve it with the slaw on a bun. Grilled shrimp with a little blackened seasoning is also nice on a bed of this slaw and is another quick dinner option.

For the slaw:

1 (14-ounce) bag coleslaw mix (I like the tri-colored, but plain is fine)

½ cup mayonnaise

3 tablespoons apple cider vinegar

3 tablespoons Sandwich Pal Weaber's horseradish sauce (if you substitute another horseradish, just taste as you go because sauces vary a lot in terms of heat)

1 tablespoon, plus 1 teaspoon, sugar

Salt and pepper to taste

For the sandwich:

6 hoagies or sausage rolls

6 andouille sausages

2 breasts from the rotisserie chicken, sliced and skin removed

For the slaw: In a small bowl, whisk together the mayonnaise, apple cider vinegar, sugar and horseradish. Salt and pepper to taste, cover and refrigerate 2 hours.

Remove breasts from the rotisserie chicken and cut into slices.

Cook andouille according to package directions. I often slice it in half so it lays flat in the bun.

I like to heat my hoagie rolls or sausage buns (I prefer sausage buns), but that is up to you. If you do heat them, I would put them in a 400 degree oven (whole, not split open), and toast for 3 minutes.

When done, place andouille in hoagie, top with sliced chicken and then add a pile of horseradish slaw. Enjoy! This is a delectable sandwich.

Gooey Chicken, Artichoke Sandwich

Serves 2-3

This chicken sandwich is crusty on the outside, gooey on the inside and packed with flavor. If you love artichoke dip, you will LOVE this because that was my inspiration for this dish. This recipe can easily be doubled and you will want to once you taste it. It's one of my favorites. I like to serve it with a side salad.

2 cups chopped rotisserie chicken breast

4 ounces cream cheese, softened

3 tablespoons mayonnaise

2 tablespoons your favorite olive tapenade (I like green olive for this)

1 cup chopped jarred artichoke hearts, drained

1 cup shredded, fresh Parmesan cheese

⅛ teaspoon Italian seasoning

Half a loaf of French or Italian bread (not baguette)

Preheat oven to 375 degrees.

Stir together chicken, cream cheese, mayonnaise, olive tapenade, artichoke hearts, Parmesan and Italian seasoning. Set aside.

Cut the bread in half and then cut it horizontally. Fill the bread with chicken mixture. If desired, add a tiny sprinkle of more Italian seasoning.

Wrap the loaf in aluminum foil and pop it in the oven for 18-20 minutes. When it's done, slice and serve.

California Chicken Sandwich with Basil Mayo

Serves 2

Easy. Easy. Easy. That sums up this sandwich. If you want something quick but with great flavor, try this. I add basil paste to the mayonnaise and then simply add chicken, avocado, tomato and a touch of garlic salt. This easy sandwich gets a big punch of flavor from the basil mayonnaise. Be sure to use good bread when making this because that is key to a great sandwich. This keeps well so it's a good choice to take on a picnic or to the office for lunch.

Tip: leftover ciabatta makes the best croutons. I buy a premade garlic butter spread from the grocery store, cut ciabatta into bite size pieces, and apply the garlic spread on three sides. Then I sprinkle on Italian seasoning and bake at 425 degrees for 5-7 minutes. These croutons are addictive and liven up a salad.

2 ciabatta rolls (or a large chunk of Italian bread)

¼ cup mayonnaise

1 ¼ teaspoons basil paste (these are the refrigerated tubes of herbs you see in the store, usually near herbs or produce)

1 avocado

1 ripe, beefsteak tomato

Dash of garlic salt

1 large rotisserie chicken breast

Mix together mayonnaise and basil paste and set aside. Slice your bread open and if the bread is thick, slightly pick out some of the bread at the bottom or top so you can layer avocado slices in there.

Then spread mayonnaise mixture inside the bread.

Slice avocado, tomato and chicken. Sprinkle garlic salt on the tomatoes. Then layer all three ingredients in the sandwich and you're done.

Grilled Chicken, Ham, Arugula and Cranberry Sandwich

Makes 4 sandwiches

I adore this quick and easy sandwich.

The creamy, sweet and tart cranberry sauce is wonderful with the spicy arugula and mellow chicken and salty, smoky ham. You don't need any fancy bread for this, just plain grocery store whole wheat works fine. You grill it like a grilled cheese.

If you have a child who is able to help in the kitchen, they can assemble the sandwich while you heat the skillet and grill the sandwiches.

It can be turned into a wrap if you're in a rush and eaten cold. In that case, simply spread the cranberry mayonnaise mixture on the inside of a whole wheat wrap. Top with ham and sliced chicken and a big handful of arugula. Roll up like you would a burrito.

8 slices whole wheat bread

2 tablespoons butter, divided

½ cup whole cranberry sauce

½ cup mayonnaise

¾ cup arugula (can substitute spinach)

8 slices of deli ham

2 rotisserie chicken breasts, cut into fourths

Pull chicken breasts off the bone and cut into fourths. You want fairly thick slices of meat.

Spread butter lightly over one side of each slice of bread.

Mix together mayonnaise and cranberry sauce and spread over opposite side of bread (not on the buttered side).

Heat a large non-stick frying pan over medium heat.

When warm, add two slices of bread, butter side down, in the pan. Add ham, chicken and arugula and then add the other piece of bread so the butter side is up (just like you would in a grilled cheese).

Press down with a spatula and when the bottom side is golden brown, flip it. Cook until the other side is golden brown and serve warm.

Chicken, Mushroom Tapenade Cheese Sandwich

Serves 3

Just wait until you taste this sandwich. Creamy Havarti melts perfectly on this sandwich which is stuffed with a homemade mushroom tapenade, chicken, sundried tomatoes and herbs, cream cheese, and then topped with salty Parmesan. It's an explosion of flavor and textures. This is fantastic with a glass of dry red wine (open the good stuff; this sandwich is worth it).

Three-fourths of French baguette

⅓ cup chopped red onion

1 teaspoon extra virgin olive oil

7 Spanish green olives

1 large portabella mushroom cap

⅓ of a small red bell pepper

½ teaspoon dried rosemary

2 tablespoons chopped sundried tomatoes

¾ cup chopped rotisserie chicken breast

3 ounces cream cheese

3 slices of Havarti

¼ cup shredded Parmesan cheese

5 basil leaves

Preheat oven to 400 degrees.

Place mushroom, green olives, red bell pepper and sundried tomatoes in a food processor and process into small pieces (like a tapenade consistency).

In a medium nonstick pan, heat the olive oil. When hot, add chopped onion and mushroom mixture and rosemary and cook for 7 minutes. Then stir in cream cheese until it is well combined and remove from heat. Stir in chopped rotisserie chicken.

Cut the baguette in half horizontally, being careful not to slice it all the way through. Then open it up and place Havarti slices on top.

Fill the sandwich with most of the mushroom mixture (there will be a little left over). Top the mushroom tapenade with Parmesan and bake the sandwich for 7 minutes (or until cheese melts and bread is toasty).

Add fresh basil to the sandwich and serve. Prepare to be WOWED.

Rosemary Chicken Salad

Serves 4 (or makes a good party appetizer)

It's hard to pinpoint which chicken salad recipe in this book is my favorite, but this is in my top 2. This recipe is so easy and fantastic. I love rosemary, which was the inspiration for this recipe (and we grow and dry rosemary every year so I had some handy). The rosemary is a huge pop of flavor.

I like to serve this on ciabatta; grilled Italian or French bread; or Ritz crackers or tortilla chips.

People rave about it every time I make it, which is pretty often. You can substitute light mayonnaise in this recipe and it's just as delicious.

Tip: For a low carb version, serve this on Bibb lettuce or thick slices of cucumber.

3 cups chopped rotisserie chicken

1/3 cup chopped red onion

2/3 cups chopped celery (about 3 stalks)

¾ cup mayonnaise

1 teaspoon red wine vinegar

1 heaping tablespoon finely minced, dried rosemary

Garlic salt to taste

Combine chicken, onion and celery and set aside.

In another bowl, mix the mayonnaise, vinegar, rosemary and garlic salt. I added ¼ teaspoon of garlic salt but I like it salty, so I would salt to taste.

Stir together both mixes and enjoy. This is better the next day so I suggest making it in advance.

Light Greek Chicken Salad

Serves 4

If you love chicken salad, but are watching your fat intake, then try my Greek version. It's a light and healthy version. It has fewer calories, less than half the fat of traditional chicken salad, and adds calcium and probiotics. You can shave more calories by using low fat yogurt – and it still tastes good.

Dill and Kalamata olives really pump up the flavor in this dish. I use garlic salt to flavor it, too. I enjoy this salad in a wrap, but you can also serve it as a salad or with pita chips as a dip.

The key is to refrigerate it at least 2 hours before serving (more is always better).

1 rotisserie chicken

4 green onions

1 stalk celery

1 cup chopped cucumber

⅓ cup chopped Kalamata olives

1 cup plain Greek yogurt (whole or low fat)

1 teaspoon dried dill weed

1 teaspoon lemon juice

Garlic salt to taste

Pepper to taste

Remove all the skin from the rotisserie chicken and discard. Then pull the meat off the bones and chop the entire chicken into pieces. Place it in a large container with a lid.

Chop onions, celery, cucumber and Kalamata olives and add to chicken.

In another bowl, stir together Greek yogurt, dill weed, lemon juice and a dose of garlic salt. Pour over chicken and stir to combine all ingredients.

Cover and refrigerate at least 2 hours. Add garlic salt and pepper to taste before serving.

Mock Muffuletta

Makes 3

A Muffuletta is a sandwich that originated with Italian immigrants in New Orleans and it's sold all over that city. Muffuletta consists of layers of olive salad, salami, ham, cheese and mortadella - which is an Italian sausage. Does it sound like a heart attack between bread? It sort of is- fatty and salty.

But there are elements I love about this sandwich which is why I created this healthier version.

Instead of mortadella, which is extremely fatty, I add chicken. I use an olive tapenade and toss it with mayonnaise which cuts the saltiness and adds a creamy flavor. I also toast this sandwich instead of eating it cold because the salami feels less fatty when it's toasted and I like melted cheese.

3 hoagies or Italian bread sliced into sandwich portions

⅓ cup mayonnaise

¼ cup green olive tapenade

6 slices salami

9 slices of deli ham

⅔ cup shredded Manchego cheese (You can substitute Swiss)

3 slices of provolone cheese

1 cup chopped rotisserie chicken breast

Dash of Italian seasoning

Preheat oven to 400 degrees.

Mix mayonnaise and olive tapenade and spread on bread until the sauces has all been used.

Divided cheeses and chicken between the hoagies and add a dash of Italian seasoning to each sandwich. Top each with two slices of salami and three slices of ham.

Bake for 5-7 minutes until cheese melts and bread is toasty. Serve immediately.

Indian Inspired Pita

Serves 4

My inspiration for this sandwich goes back to my childhood. When I was in fifth grade, I lived in the country formerly known as Zaire. One of my classmates was Indian and she loved American food; I loved Indian food. So each day, I'd swap my chocolate pudding or Doritos for her mom's homemade samosas. I'd trade my pizza for her lamb burgers. Unlike American burgers which are garnished with lettuce and tomato, her mom always stacked cucumbers on top. So that was my inspiration for this sandwich that only takes 10 minutes to assemble.

One of my favorite store-bought sauces is SWAD Coriander Chutney, which is excellent on Samosas. SWAD is the brand name and if you can't find it locally, you can order it online or substitute another coriander chutney. I mix the chutney with mayonnaise, toss the sauce over chopped chicken, add cucumbers and lettuce and stuff it into a whole wheat pita pocket.

It's easy, delicious and refreshing. While this is my favorite way to eat the sandwich, I have a dill variation. Instead of chutney, I add 1 teaspoon dried dill or 2-3 teaspoons fresh dill. Decrease mayonnaise to ¼ cup and add 2 tablespoons sour cream. I still top it with cucumbers and lettuce. The cucumbers are a wonderful compliment to the dill.

This recipe serves 4 but can easily be halved if you just want to make it for yourself. It's one of my 10 minute recipes.

4 cups chopped rotisserie chicken

⅔ cup mayonnaise

4 teaspoons SWAD coriander chutney

Salt and pepper to taste.

1 large cucumber

Green leaf lettuce

4 pita pockets

Chop chicken and set aside. Mix together mayonnaise and chutney. Stir in chicken. Taste and adjust salt and pepper.

Slice cucumbers and stuff chicken, cucumber and lettuce in pita pockets. Enjoy.

Main Courses

Chicken, Ranch, Black Bean Quesadilla

Serves 4

8 ounces whipped cream cheese, at room temperature

1 tablespoon dry Ranch salad dressing mix

½ cup corn, drained

2 tablespoons chopped black olives

½ cup black beans, drained

1 tablespoon, plus 1 teaspoon of chopped red onion

⅓ cup chunky salsa (it must be chunky)

1 cup chopped chicken

2 cups shredded Mexican-style cheese

4 (6-inch) flour tortillas

Guacamole or extra salsa to serve (optional)

Preheat oven to 400 degrees.

Mix together cream cheese and Ranch dressing until thoroughly combined. Then, stir in corn, black olives, black beans, onion, salsa and chicken.

Place mixture in half of a tortilla and top each with ½ cup of cheese. Fold the tortilla over to make a half moon.

Bake for 6-8 minutes. Tortilla will be crispy.

Lettuce Wraps with Sweet Peanut Sauce

Serves 2

These lettuce wraps are easy, healthy and perfect on a hot summer day.

They are versatile, too. You can add any vegetable you like. I have swapped soba noodles for rice noodles, added snow peas, shiitake mushrooms, sliced daikon and poached asparagus.

The peanut sauce comes together in minutes. It doesn't have any ginger, but if you want to add some, start with 1/8 teaspoon and go from there because ginger is potent.

There's hardly any cooking in this recipe, so it's perfect for people who don't want to spend much time in the kitchen.

Tip: Since you have to prepare rice noodles and slice vegetables, this would be a good time to double the amount of veggies you slice and use the other half for a stir-fry tomorrow night. You can also double the rice noodle recipe and serve the stir-fry over those noodles.

2 rotisserie chicken breasts, sliced

8-10 butter lettuce leaves, washed and dried

Two handfuls fresh cilantro

½ cup shredded carrots

1 ounce rice noodles

Sesame oil or your favorite Asian dressing

1 cucumber, sliced thin

1 green onion, sliced thin

Sliced bell pepper (optional)

For the sauce:

¼ cup creamy peanut butter

½ cup boiling water

1 tablespoon brown sugar (do not make this

heaping or it will be too sweet)

1 ½ teaspoons fresh lime juice

1 teaspoon soy sauce

First: Cook your rice noodles according to package directions. When they are done, drizzle with sesame oil or your favorite Asian salad dressing such as Sesame Ginger. *Continued on page 82*

Rice noodles are fairly flavorless, so this will add some depth of flavor and prevent them from sticking together. If you want them to cool quickly, place them in a metal bowl and pop it in the fridge.

Slice all the vegetables and place them on a large platter or divide between two plates.

Remove the skin from the chicken and place it on a plate.

Make your peanut sauce.

For the sauce: Stir all ingredients together until they are combined. The water must be very hot to dissolve the peanut butter.

You can also make this on a stovetop in a small pot, but it needs to cool before serving because the peanut butter will separate and become too thin while piping hot.

Make your own wraps by placing desired toppings in the lettuce leaves and then either topping it with or dipping in peanut sauce. Sprinkle with sliced green onion and eat.

Quick Chicken Marsala

Serves 2

2 tablespoons canola oil

Half a large red onion

1 tablespoon flour

8 ounces sliced mushrooms

1 cup chicken stock

1 garlic clove, chopped

⅛ teaspoon dried oregano

⅛ teaspoon Italian seasoning

2 rotisserie chicken breasts

⅔ cup Marsala wine

¼ cup heavy cream

Salt and pepper to taste

Couscous or instant rice for serving

Place onion in food processor and chop.

Heat oil in a large skillet over medium heat. When hot, add onion and saute 4 minutes. Then, add flour and mushrooms and cook another 5 minutes. Add some salt and pepper to your vegetables as they cook.

While that cooks, remove chicken breasts from rotisserie chicken and cut into four pieces.

Add stock, garlic, oregano, Italian seasoning and chicken breasts and increase heat to medium-high. Cook 5 minutes until stock reduces and thickens. Add Marsala and cook 1 minute and stir in the heavy cream at the end.

Serve immediately over couscous or rice. I prefer couscous.

Jordanian Inspired Chicken in Filo Dough

Serves 5

My initial inspiration for this recipe was a Moroccan filo pie, but it was extremely complicated and used tons of spices.

So when I started to simplify this in my head, I remembered a dish I learned to make when I took a cooking class in Jordan. I went there a few years ago to visit Petra, which is a spectacular site. In the cooking class we made this delicious chicken seasoned with coriander, pepper, cinnamon and nutmeg. It's one of my favorite chicken dishes to this day.

So I combined both culinary inspirations and came up with this dish, which is excellent. I am thrilled with the results. There wasn't a bite left.

1 tablespoon canola oil

1 very large red onion (or two medium)

1 ½ teaspoons ground coriander

1 ½ teaspoons cinnamon

¾ teaspoon ground nutmeg

¼ teaspoon pepper

¼ teaspoon salt (plus more to taste)

2 cups chopped rotisserie chicken

½ cup pomegranate-infused dried cranberries (or substitute raisins)

1 tablespoon tomato paste

½ cup chicken broth

1 roll of Filo dough

½ cup melted butter for brushing

Thaw filo dough according to package directions.

Preheat oven to 400 degrees.

Slice onion and set aside. In a large pan, heat oil over medium heat, then add onion and spices and sauté for 5 minutes. Add the chicken and cook 5 more minutes. Add dried cranberries, tomato paste and broth. Cover dish and cook for 5 minutes. Taste and add more salt if needed. Remove lid and pop mixture in the refrigerator for 5 minutes to cool slightly.

Use a deep-dish pie pan and layer several layers of filo dough on the bottom with the sides hanging over the pie pan. Brush with melted butter. Do this until you've used half the dough. Fill the filo dough with chicken mixture. Place the rest of the filo dough, adding two sheets at a time and quickly brushing with butter, until you have added all the dough and tuck it all in the sides of the pie pan, like a little present.

Brush with remaining butter. Bake for 20-25 minutes or until golden on top. Cool for 5 minutes before slicing.

This dish can be served as an appetizer or main course. It pairs well with a Riesling or a beer.

Southwest Style Stuffed Peppers

Serves 4

I've always loved stuffed peppers, but making a batch can take hours. This is one of the easiest versions of stuffed peppers I've come up with. Instead of rice, I use hominy and puree it in the food processor. It adds bulk, holds the dish together and offers a delicious, deep corn flavor.

I then use rotisserie chicken, cumin and picante sauce. Of course, a good dose of cilantro and cheese is wonderful, too. These peppers are assembled in about 10 minutes and baked for 15-20 minutes. The peppers are still crisp, which I love. Vegetables retain more nutrients when they are not overcooked. This is a perfect dinner for a busy night.

1 (15-ounce) can hominy

2 teaspoons cumin seed

1 cup picante sauce

1 rotisserie chicken, chopped and de-skinned

⅔ cup canned black beans, drained

⅓ cup chopped cilantro

2 cups shredded cheddar or Mexican-blend cheese

Garlic salt to taste

4 bell peppers of assorted colors (red and yellow are my favorite)

Preheat oven to 425 degrees.

Drain hominy and place it in the food processor with cumin seed. Pulse until semi-smooth, then pour in a large bowl. Add picante sauce, chicken, black beans and cilantro. Add 1 cup of cheese. Stir to thoroughly combine the mixture. Set aside.

Cut bell peppers in half and remove seeds and any veins. Stuff each half with the mixture and top with remaining cheese.

Cover with aluminum foil and bake 15 minutes, then remove foil and bake another 5 minutes. Peppers will still be crisp.

Puff Pastry filled with Chicken, Artichokes and Cheese

Serves 2-3

Golden, buttery puff pastry is wrapped around chunks of artichokes and chicken tossed with creamy mayonnaise, cheese, a hint of salty bacon, and accented with Italian seasoning. It's lovely.

Serve it with grilled asparagus and salad or sautéed spinach on the side.

1 puff pastry (Pepperidge Farm is my favorite)

1 cup drained artichokes

1 cup chopped boneless, skinless rotisserie chicken breast

⅓ cup shredded Asiago cheese (could substitute Parmesan if you can't find Asiago)

⅔ cup shredded mozzarella cheese

½ cup mayonnaise

½ teaspoon Italian seasoning

2 tablespoons crumbled cooked bacon or real bacon pieces (optional)

Dash of garlic salt

Parchment paper

Preheat oven to 400 degrees.

Drain artichokes, pat with a paper towel to dry and roughly chop artichokes. Stir together artichokes, chicken, cheeses, mayonnaise, bacon and Italian seasoning. Top with a dash of garlic salt.

Lay a piece of parchment paper on a baking sheet, this will help prevent the puff pastry from sticking.

Unfold puff pastry and remove the paper. The pastry will naturally be divided in thirds and all you want to do is fill that middle third with the chicken mixture. So carefully spoon all the mixture down the center of the pastry and fold the sides up and over to seal. Dip your fingers in water and seal the edges so the cheese doesn't bubble out.

Bake 18-22 minutes. Remove from oven and allow to rest 5 minutes before slicing. Enjoy with a glass of Sauvignon Blanc or Chardonnay; or any red from a Pinot to Cabernet Sauvignon.

Barbecue Chicken Quesadillas with Corn and Bacon

Serves 1

For this easy quesadilla, I simply shred rotisserie chicken meat, toss it in my favorite barbecue sauce, nestle it in a tortilla with cheese, red onion, corn, cilantro, bacon pieces and toss it in the skillet. It takes minutes to cook up. These quesadillas are a great snack, too. My recipe is for a single serving, but it's easy to double or triple.

Tip: I really like fresh corn in this dish, but you could save yourself time by using 2-3 tablespoons of canned corn that has been thoroughly drained and patted dry with a paper towel. The Mexicorn blend is particularly good in this dish.

1 ear of corn

1 (10-inch) flour tortilla

½ a rotisserie chicken breast

1 tablespoon barbecue sauce, plus more for dipping

1 tablespoon cilantro

1 ½ teaspoon finely minced red onion

1 tablespoon real bacon pieces

About ½ cup shredded Taco cheese (use desired amount of cheese)

Place the ear of corn in its husk in the microwave and cook for 3 ½ minutes. When cool enough to handle, strip off the husk and cut the cob in half. Then cut the corn off half the cob and set it aside. Save the rest of the cob for another use.

Tear chicken breast off the chicken, discard the skin and shred the meat with your hands. Toss it in barbecue sauce and set aside.

Chop onion and cilantro and set aside. Have all your ingredients handy before you heat the pan because you will assemble this in the pan and it cooks quickly.

Spray a large nonstick pan with cooking spray and heat it over medium heat. When hot, add the tortilla shell and hold half of it up to make a half moon. Fill the bottom half with cheese first and then the remaining ingredients. Close the shell so it looks like a half moon. Cook 2-3 minute per side.

Serve with barbecue sauce for dipping, if desired.

Chicken, Bacon and Gorgonzola Flatbread

Makes 2 flatbreads

Flatbreads are all the rage in restaurants but there's no reason to pay a premium to enjoy one. You can crank out restaurant-quality flatbreads at home in no time. This one is definitely restaurant quality. It's bubbly, creamy, bacon-goodness.

It's topped with bits of tart apple that provide a nice contrast in terms of texture and flavor. This dish is divine and great with a glass of red wine. I don't usually like blue cheese, but Gorgonzola is much lighter than many other varieties and this doesn't even taste like blue cheese. Really, this flatbread is incredible.

Tip: Slice this into pieces and serve it as an appetizer for a party or serve it with a side salad for dinner. It makes two flatbreads, which could feed 3-4 with a side salad.

1 (8.8 ounce) package (which contains 2 flatbreads) of Stonefire Tandoori Baked Original Naan

5 ounces cream cheese, softened

⅓ cup real bacon pieces or chopped bacon, plus 1 teaspoon (do not use bacon bits)

2 tablespoons heavy whipping cream

¼ teaspoon garlic powder

½ cup Gorgonzola crumbles

1 ¼ cups chopped rotisserie chicken

⅔ cup shredded mozzarella cheese

1 Granny Smith apple

Preheat oven to 400 degrees.

Stir together cream cheese, bacon, heavy whipping cream, garlic powder and Gorgonzola. Set aside.

Remove the breasts from the rotisserie chicken and chop those. Finely mince the Granny Smith apple and set aside.

When oven is preheated, spread half the cream cheese mixture on each flatbread. Sprinkle half the chicken on each flatbread and top with mozzarella cheese.

Bake for 9 minutes. Then sprinkle with the apple and serve.

Creole Fried Rice

Serves 3-4

I love fried rice and this is my Southern version.

The rice is flavored with Cajun seasoning, oregano, andouille, chicken, and a "Trinity" that is still crunchy, adding depth to the texture.

If you're not familiar with the "Trinity" or "Holy Trinity" term, it's a combination of onion, bell pepper and celery. This is the foundation of Cajun and Creole cooking and a staple in our house. I am married to a Louisiana man.

There are a lot of differences between Cajun and Creole cooking, but the biggest one is tomatoes. You will notice I called this dish "Creole Fried Rice," and that's because I use tomatoes in it. If you're down South and have a jambalaya or gumbo with tomatoes, you're eating a Creole-style dish.

Another big difference is that Cajun food is considered to be more from the country. Creole cuisine is considered more city food.

Here's a very condensed history. The word Cajun comes from "les Acadians," who were French colonists who settled in Canada. After British conquest of that area, those French descendants settled in south Louisiana in the region now called Acadiana. This was a swampy region and what evolved in terms of food was incredible fare using local resources. Rice is a staple and so are spices and seasonings. There are a lot of one-pot dishes and just down-home comfort.

The Creoles lived in New Orleans and were upper-class descendants of settlers. The influences in that cuisine were largely Spanish, French and African, so there's more fusion in this cooking. Also, the Creoles had more money to buy ingredients and to import ingredients, so dishes can be a little more complicated.

In general, I prefer Cajun food, and I use more Cajun ingredients. Of course, this is an oversimplification and both styles of food have evolved.

I can say it's a big compliment that my husband loved this dish – although it's my Creole version, not Cajun.

Be careful when using Cajun seasoning in this recipe because a lot of grocery-store brands are terribly salty. I use Joe's Stuff, which I discovered at the New Orleans School of Cooking.

Just be sure you taste your Cajun seasoning before adding it to the dish. *Continued on page 96*

This fried rice came together in about 15 minutes, which is perfect on a busy weeknight (and it was a busy weeknight when I created this).

It's a great way to use up leftover white rice or, if you plan ahead and are making rice on Monday, make a double batch and have leftover rice ready to go on Tuesday.

1 teaspoon canola oil

1 medium red onion, chopped

1 cup chopped celery

2/3 cup chopped green bell pepper

2 andouille sausages

2 cups day-old rice

1 cup chopped rotisserie chicken

1/4 teaspoon Cajun seasoning

3/4 teaspoon oregano

1 cup canned tomatoes with celery, onions and peppers

Chop all vegetables (or use a food processor). If you're using a food processor, coarsely chop the vegetables.

Slice andouille in half and then chop into bite-size pieces.

In a large skillet, heat oil over medium-high heat. When it's hot, add onions and cook 2 minutes. Then add celery and andouille and cook 5 minutes, stirring occasionally.

While that cooks, chop your chicken and set aside.

Add bell pepper and cook 1 minute (you want it to still be crisp). Now add rice, chicken, Cajun seasoning, oregano and tomatoes to the dish and cook another 3 minutes. You want to toss the rice so it's coated in tomatoes, but don't over-stir the rice or it will become gummy.

Taste and add salt and pepper, if needed.

Goat Cheese, Chicken and Tri-Pepper Quesadilla

Serves 1

The charm of the quesadilla is it's quick, easy, versatile and delicious. It's portable, so you can eat it on the go as a snack, but also filling enough to enjoy it for dinner.

If you're watching your carb intake, you can substitute a high-protein, low-carb wrap for the tortilla shell.

The goat cheese quesadilla is tossed with green salsa which is an amazing combination. It's one of my favorite quesadillas as the creamy, tangy goat cheese pairs nicely with a trio of bell peppers. Goat cheese is also less fattening and I like the fact that my recipe includes veggies. This is a single serving recipe, so it's perfect for a snack or someone who lives solo.

Tip: when making a quesadilla that is stuffed with other ingredients, cook it cheese side down first so it has a chance to melt and the cheese doesn't fall out when you flip it.

Use a nonstick pan or a skillet to make quesadillas. If you're feeding a crowd, a pancake griddle works well to cook several at the same time (if you have a family, a griddle is a great choice).

Tip: Goat cheese and green salsa make a wonderful party dip. Mix 4 ounce chevre with ¾ cup green salsa and serve with tortilla chips.

1 medium size tortilla

Cooking spray

⅓ cup of assorted sliced bell peppers - red, green and yellow or orange

¼ cup of soft chevre (goat cheese in a log)

1 ½ tablespoons green salsa

Dash of ground cumin

⅓ cup sliced or chopped rotisserie chicken breast

Guacamole or green salsa for serving

First, slice assorted bell peppers and heat a nonstick skillet coated with cooking spray over medium-high heat. When hot, add the bell peppers and cook 3-5 minutes until they reach desired tenderness. Salt the peppers and remove from heat.

In a bowl, stir together the goat cheese and green salsa until combined. Then spread the mixture over half of a tortilla. Top with chicken and bell peppers. Then sprinkle a dash of ground cumin on the other side of the tortilla and fold over to make a half moon.

Spray a nonstick skillet with cooking spray and heat it over medium heat. Add the folded tortilla and cook about 2-3 minutes per side, until slightly crisp. Slice and serve with green salsa or guacamole.

Mexican Lasagna

Serves 6-8

This is one of my all-time most popular recipes. People gobble it up. This dish is layers of corn tortillas, covered in a mix of black beans, chicken, salsa, cumin and cheese. It's delectable.

This calls for 4 cups of rotisserie chicken, which is the whole chicken. If you don't like dark meat and want only white, you will need to buy 2 chickens and just use the breast off both (but really, the flavors in the sauce cover up the dark meat).

This makes a large batch (13" x 9" pan), but the recipe can easily be halved. This is an economical dish when entertaining and absolutely delicious. This lasagna explodes with flavor.

If you're watching your weight, you can use less cheese in this dish by skipping the middle layer of cheese. This has such powerful flavors, you really won't miss it too much.

Tip: You will have leftover corn tortillas, which you could use to make my Chicken Tortilla Soup or Quick Chicken Enchiladas. Corn tortillas freeze well, so if you won't use them for a few weeks, you can freeze them.

1 package soft yellow corn tortillas (you will not use them all)

1 tablespoon canola oil

1 very large yellow onion

2 teaspoons ground cumin

1 ½ teaspoons cumin seed

1 green bell pepper

1 red bell pepper

1 can seasoned black beans, drained

4 cups chopped skinless rotisserie chicken (1 whole chicken or 2 if just using breast meat)

2 ¾ cups chunky salsa or picante sauce (that's more than a regular-size jar, so buy a big jar or 2 regular ones)

Dash of garlic salt

½ cup cilantro (optional)

3 ½ cups of shredded Mexican-cheese blend or Taco cheese

Preheat oven to 400 degrees.

Put onion through a food processor and chop bell peppers and set aside.

If you plan to use cilantro, gather the leaves in a bunch and cut off stems at the base of where the leaves start. Chop the leaves and set aside.

Chop your chicken and set aside. *Continued on page 100*

In a large skillet, heat oil over medium heat. When oil is hot, add onion, cumin powder and cumin seed and cook 6 minutes. Then add chopped bell peppers and cook 2 minutes. Stir in beans, chicken, salsa and a dash of garlic salt and cook 2 minutes. If you plan to add cilantro, stir it in now. Turn off heat and let mixture rest.

Spray a 13" x 9" pan with cooking spray. Line the bottom with corn tortillas, overlapping in spots so that the bottom is covered. I tear tortillas into desired sizes to make them fit. You will not use the entire package; you just want enough to make layers.

Take half your chicken mixture and spread it evenly over the first layer of tortillas. Top that mixture with about 40 percent of your cheese. You want a little extra cheese on top. Then repeat and make another layer of tortillas over the mixture. Make sure it's all covered, even if you overlap tortillas. Then top that with the rest of the chicken mixture. Cover chicken with remaining cheese.

Bake for 15-20 minutes or until cheese bubbles. Slice and serve. I hope you enjoy this; I absolutely love it.

Moroccan Chicken with Couscous

Serves 4

This dish is healthy, but packed with flavor and nutrients. The orange zest and red bell pepper offer a good dose of Vitamin C. It's low fat and comes together so quickly. I have served it to company and they raved about it. A Zinfandel would be a good wine choice to pair with this dish.

Tip: You can zest the other half of the orange and add it to balsamic vinegar. Add a dash of dried rosemary and allow it to infuse overnight. Then mix the vinegar with olive oil and dip bread in the mixture. Eat it as a snack as you prepare dinner tomorrow. The zest adds amazing flavor and is loaded with antioxidants.

2 teaspoons canola oil

1 medium red onion

1 red bell pepper

1 heaping teaspoon cumin seed

½ teaspoon ground cinnamon

⅓ cup Pomegranate-infused dried cranberries

1 teaspoon olive oil

1 (5.7-ounce) box garlic-flavored couscous

½ cup chopped cilantro

3 cups chopped rotisserie chicken

Zest from half an orange

This one-pot dish is absolutely delicious and comes together in 20 minutes. It's packed with flavor.

Chop onion and red bell pepper and set aside. You can use a food processor; just keep the bell pepper a little chunkier.

Remove skin and chop chicken breasts and either leg or thigh meat. Depending on the size of the bird, this should yield enough chicken.

Take about 2/3 of a bunch of cilantro and chop it. Set aside.

Zest your orange and set aside.

In a large nonstick pot, heat oil over medium heat. When hot, add onion and cook until almost tender. Add red bell pepper, cumin and cinnamon and cook 2 minutes.

Then add as much water as required to make the couscous (it will say on the back of the box, and you're making the entire box; add flavor packet and dried cranberries. *Continued on page 102*

Basically, you are making it according to package directions, but you cut the amount of olive oil in half because you already used canola in the vegetables.

When water comes to a boil, add couscous, stir, cover with a tight lid and let it rest for 5 minutes.

NOTE: If your chicken is fresh from the store, you will add it at the end. If it's been refrigerated, then you should add it to the couscous before you put the lid on to allow it to warm up.

When couscous is ready, fluff with a fork and toss in cilantro, chopped chicken and orange zest.

Serve immediately.

NOTE: if you don't like using flavored couscous, you can use plain, but I suggest cooking it in reduced-sodium chicken broth instead of water. Use the same measurements.

BLT Alfredo

Serves 4-6

How do you make creamy Alfredo better? Just add bacon. I adore this dish. It's seriously com-forting on a winter night. A BLT sandwich was my inspiration for this pasta. The spinach subs in for lettuce and the tomatoes add freshness to this dish.

Tip: You will have leftover tomatoes and bacon pieces, which are delicious in scrambled eggs in the morning. It's a good way to use some leftovers.

Both breasts from rotisserie chicken

8 ounces angel hair pasta

¼ cup butter

1 garlic clove

1 cup heavy whipping cream

1 cup fresh Parmesan cheese

½ cup fresh spinach leaves

1/3 cup real bacon pieces

2 tablespoons chopped fresh flat leaf parsley

2 tablespoons fresh basil

½ cup sliced grape tomatoes

Salt and pepper to taste

This dish comes together quickly. Put your water on to boil for pasta.

Then remove the chicken breasts and the skin. Chop chicken into chunks and set aside.

Slice tomatoes in half, slice basil, and chop parsley and set aside.

Cook pasta according to directions for al dente noodles. In a large deep skillet, heat butter and garlic for 1 minute. Add heavy cream and cook over me-dium heat for 5 minutes. By the time this is done, your pasta should be ready. Drain pasta, but reserve ¼ cup of liquid that the pasta cooked in.

Add pasta liquid, pasta, cheese and bacon, and cook 1 minute until noodles are coated and mix-ture thickens. Then stir in remaining ingredients, toss to coat and turn off heat. Allow to rest for 5 minutes before serving (the sauce will thicken a little more).

Chicken Pot Pie with Refrigerator Biscuits

My drop biscuit chicken pot pie is a favorite in our house. It's totally comforting with warm biscuits baked on top to soak up the juices in the dish. I use the refrigerator biscuits, so that saves time.

It's packed with vegetables and I use whole milk instead of cream to lighten it up. A dash of thyme and bay leaves lifts the flavor in this dish.

It's a simple recipe, but will take longer than my usual recipes because you have to bake it for 15-20 minutes. But hey, I find that's the perfect time to clean up and set the table.

2 tablespoons canola oil	Salt and pepper to taste
1 ½ cups chopped yellow onion	1 ½ cups chicken stock
2 cups chopped celery	3 cups whole milk
2 tablespoons flour	1 ½ cups frozen peas and carrots
2 bay leaves	4 cups chopped rotisserie chicken meat
¼ teaspoon thyme leaves	2 packages small refrigerated biscuits

This makes a large batch, but you could halve the recipe and make it in an 8 x 8 dish. If you're a family, you will want the larger version because it's delicious and you will probably eat more than you expect. This is the quintessential winter dish—down-home and comforting. It's a great recipe to make on a Sunday night.

Chop all ingredients and set aside.

Preheat oven to 400 degrees.

In a large pot, heat the oil over medium heat. When hot, add the onion, celery, flour, bay leaves, thyme and cook for 5-7 minutes. Stir to be sure the flour doesn't burn. Then add a dash of salt and pepper.

Add chicken broth, milk, peas and carrots, and cook 7 more minutes, stirring frequently. The sauce should be thickening. Add your chicken and cook about 3 more minutes.

If sauce is not thickening to your liking, remove ½ cup of liquid and whisk in 1 teaspoon cornstarch. Then whisk that back into the mix and turn heat up slightly. It will thicken. Keep in mind though, this is meant to be slightly soupy so that you can soak it up with the biscuits on top.

When done, pour into a 13 x 11 baking dish. Top with 15-20 refrigerator biscuits (these are the small ones). Bake for 15-20 minutes, until biscuits are golden.

Quick Chicken Enchiladas

Serves 5

These enchiladas are on the dry side, which is what I like. If you like really wet, swimming-in-sauce enchiladas, then buy two cans of sauce or a large one.

1 rotisserie chicken

⅔ cup chunky salsa

1 teaspoon ground cumin

1 (10-ounce) jar green or red enchilada sauce (use 19-ounce size if you like really wet enchiladas)

Refried beans

2 cups shredded Mexican-blend cheese, or Taco cheese

10-12 corn tortillas

Tomatoes, sour cream, guacamole to garnish

Preheat oven to 400 degrees.

Debone and de-skin your chicken. Then pull off all the meat and shred it with your hands and place in a large bowl.

Add salsa, cumin and half the jar of enchilada sauce and stir to coat. Taste and adjust seasoning if you'd like.

Spray a glass pan with cooking spray. Spread about 1-2 tablespoons of refried beans on each tortilla.

Fill each tortilla with chicken and a sprinkle of cheese. Roll shut and place face-down on the pan. Repeat until you've used all your chicken. Then top with remaining cheese and drizzle the rest of the enchilada sauce over the dish.

Bake for 20-25 minutes. Serve garnished with tomatoes, guacamole, sour cream and any desired toppings.

Desserts

I am a big believer that dessert should knock my socks off.

Life is too short – and dessert is too high in calories-- to settle for a mediocre end to a meal.

So when I create something sweet, I want to wow and be wowed. These desserts accomplish that mission. And no, they don't contain rotisserie chicken.

Sweets are one of my specialties and even though this book is dedicated to chicken, I had to include seven amazing desserts.

Why seven? Well, I am superstitious and seven has always been my good luck number: I was born in 1977; started dating my husband on the 17th; married on the 7th; had a child on the 17th, and on and on. So it just seemed right to end the book with seven delectable desserts. I am hoping it will bring us both good luck. Even if it doesn't, I hope it will be a pleasure to try these. I tried to offer a good mix from a cheesecake to a lemon dessert to a delectable Five-minute pumpkin mousse.

I love all these recipes, but my favorites are probably the Lemon-Misu and warm Chocolate, Peanut Butter Trifle.

The Lemon-Misu is layers of lemon cookies, lemon curd whipped with mascarpone cheese and whipped topping and strawberries marinated in sherry. Talk about a perfect spring and summer dessert.

For the cooler months, I can't get enough of my warm Chocolate, Peanut Butter Trifle which only takes -10 minutes to prepare so you can whip it up any time. It is layers of pound cake, warm two-ingredient peanut butter sauce, warm two-ingredient chocolate sauce and whipped topping. The flavor is so outstanding your guests will never believe the recipe is this simple. You can substitute real whipped cream on any dessert; I use whipped topping because it's faster and has less fat.

I hope you enjoy these delectable desserts. There's at least one for every season.

Warm Chocolate, Peanut Butter Trifle

Serves 6-8

Trifles are one of my favorite desserts to serve at a party because they are easy, beautiful, delicious and feed a crowd. Trifles are usually served chilled, but this one is warm, which is perfect for a cold night. The chocolate and peanut butter just melt in your mouth. It's divine.

It comes together in about 10 minutes which is amazing for a dessert. It's sure to be a crowd pleaser. I adore peanut butter and chocolate combinations and this one is exceptional.

1 large store bought pound cake (an angel cake will work, but you need a whole cake, not a half size)

½ cup creamy peanut butter

⅔ cup sweetened condensed milk

2 tablespoons hot water

⅔ cup half and half

2 cups semi-sweet chocolate chips (mini chips will melt faster)

1 (8-ounce) container of extra creamy whipped topping

Cut the cake into 1 or 2 inch pieces and set aside. You want to do this before you make the sauces because those are served warm.

Layer half the cake pieces in a trifle dish or deep bowl.

For the peanut butter sauce: In a small saucepan over medium-heat, whisk together peanut butter, sweetened condensed milk and water until the peanut butter dissolves. Add 1 more tablespoon of water if the sauce is too thick. Lower heat to low until serving.

For the chocolate sauce: In a small, nonstick pot, heat the half and half over medium heat until bubbles start to form around the edge of the pan. Immediately whisk in chocolate chips and reduce heat to low and stir until chips are dissolved and chocolate is glossy.

Immediately, pour half the chocolate sauce over the cake and top that with half the peanut butter sauce.

Then add second layer of cake and top with chocolate sauce and peanut butter sauce. Cover the top with whipped topping and serve immediately.

Pumpkin Butter Cheesecake

Serves 6

This dessert is perfect for people who don't like excessively sweet treats. Creamy cheesecake is swirled together with pumpkin butter making this a wonderful fall and winter dessert. Plus, it's a snap to make.

Tip: You will have leftover pumpkin butter after this recipe and a great way to use it is to blend it with 1 cup vanilla ice cream, ½ cup milk and 1/3 cup pumpkin butter to create a pumpkin butter shake. For a different twist on this recipe, you can also substitute apple butter for pumpkin butter.

1 (9-inch) prepared graham cracker crust

12 ounces softened cream cheese (make sure it's room temperature)

⅓ cup sugar

2 eggs

1 teaspoon vanilla extract

⅓ cup pumpkin butter

*Date Lady Caramel Sauce for serving

Preheat oven to 350 degrees.

Beat cream cheese until fluffy. Add sugar and beat until combined. Then add one egg at a time so each is incorporated. Pour 2/3 of the mixture into graham cracker crust.

Mix pumpkin butter into leftover 1/3 of the filling and then pour that over cheesecake. Swirl together.

Bake 35-45 minutes or until center is set, try to take it out before cracks form. Cool on the counter for an hour and then refrigerate until serving.

When it's time to serve, drizzle with the Date Lady Caramel sauce.

*Date Lady products are made in Springfield and the line includes vegan sauces and dates. For recipes or to see where you can buy them: https://ilovedatelady.com/

Lemon-Misu

Serves 6

Heavenly – that's the best way to describe this dessert. I adore lemon desserts, and this one was inspired by tiramisu in that I use cookies and layers of mascarpone cheese that has been whipped with lemon curd and whipped topping. Between these layers are sherry marinated strawberries. This is truly a special, unique and delectable dessert.

It's light and perfect for spring, summer or a baby shower. It's a special occasion dessert.

⅓ cup sherry

1 ¼ cup sliced strawberries

10 ounces lemon curd

1 (8-ounce) container mascarpone cheese, at room temperature.

1 (8-ounce) container whipped topping

*2 packages Lemonia cookies (or any flat, lemon cookie)

*If you can't find these cookies, which are flat lemon biscuit type cookies, you can substitute any thin lemon cookie. I've bought the Dollar Store brand and they were fine. Do not use cream filled cookies through, I tried that and it was a big failure because those cookies don't get soft. The Girl Scouts make an incredible lemon cookie and if you have those around, that would be excellent in this recipe, too. You will have leftover cookies; unfortunately, you need just a little more than one package for this recipe so there's a lot left in the second package.

Rinse, hull and slice strawberries, and then place in a shallow bowl and cover with the sherry. Set aside for 30 minutes.

Next, mix together lemon curd, mascarpone cheese and half the container of whipped topping.

Place a layer of lemon cookies in the bottom of your 8 x 8 inch pan. Be sure to cover the entire bottom even if you need to break cookies in half.

Spread half the lemon curd mixture over the cookies. Add another layer of cookies and top that with the strawberries. Pour the juices from the strawberry/sherry mixture over the layer of cookies.

Spread remaining lemon curd mixture over the strawberries and top that with remaining whipped topping. Cover and refrigerate for at least 4 hours before serving to allow the cookies to soften. This can be made a day in advance. The cookies will continue to soften the longer it stays in the refrigerator.

Pina Colada Trifle
(in honor of Uncle Floyd)

Serves 8

I invented this recipe in honor of the late Floyd Mahon, who was like an uncle to me (and so many others).

Floyd died from colon cancer. He was one of the best men I've ever known, and ever will know. I say that with certainty because he was one of those rare, exceptional people who had the ability to make everyone laugh, and make everyone feel special. You didn't have to know him long to feel like a longtime friend. He was a character.

Because of that legacy of a life well lived, his family throws Floyd-fest each year in honor of him. This year, the theme was Cancun, which was Floyd's favorite place.

Keeping the Cancun theme in mind, I whipped up this dessert in honor of Floyd. Trifles are one of my favorite desserts because they are easy, pretty, creamy, versatile and feed a crowd. And of course, who doesn't enjoy sipping a Pina Colada on a beach in Mexico? This dessert just seemed like him – fun, sweet, tropical and different.

1 white cake made according to package directions

¼ cup dark rum

2 boxes of instant coconut pudding

1 ¼ cups coconut milk (use the refrigerated type, not the canned)

2 ⅔ cups half and half (can substitute regular milk)

1 teaspoon rum extract

2 cups finely chopped fresh pineapple

1 (16-ounce) tub of extra creamy whipped topping

1 cup shredded sweet coconut

Bake cake according to package directions and 5 minutes after you remove it from the oven, brush it with rum. Set aside.

Empty two packages of coconut pudding and whisk together with coconut milk, half and half and rum extract. Whisk until well combined, then cover and refrigerate.

Peel and chop the pineapple into small bits.

To assemble the trifle, break up half the cake and place it in the bottom of a bowl or trifle dish. Top with half the coconut pudding, half the pineapple and a layer of whipped topping.

Then repeat the process to create the second layer of the trifle, and top it with whipped topping and shredded coconut. Cover and chill 2 hours before serving.

Five-minute Pumpkin Mousse

Makes 20 (2-ounce) servings

If you only try one new pumpkin recipe this year, let it be this mousse.

Don't let the word "mousse" intimidate you — this is as easy as it gets: It takes five minutes and has five ingredients. You simply whisk together sweetened condensed milk, canned pumpkin, pumpkin pie spice and whipped topping, then serve it with gingersnap cookies for dipping (although the velvety mousse is delicious on its own).

I've created a variety of pumpkin mousse recipes throughout the years, but this is my best. My husband told me he could "bathe in it."

This recipe will be a winner this holiday season. It's even better after a few hours of refrigeration, but it can be served immediately, too.

1 (14-ounce) can sweetened condensed milk

1 (15-ounce) can pumpkin puree

1 teaspoon pumpkin pie spice

1 (8-ounce) tub of whipped topping, defrosted

Mini gingersnap cookies to garnish

Beat or stir together sweetened condensed milk, pumpkin, pumpkin pie spice and whipped topping, until combined. Pour mixture into 2-ounce glasses and top with a gingersnap cookie. Serve immediately.

Tips for other serving options: If you have a smaller crowd and want to serve larger portions, you can serve mousse in wine glasses with or without a cookie. You can also crumble cookies and put them on top. Sugar cookies or vanilla wafers also pair well with this mousse.

A pretty serving option for a crowd is to buy a baking pumpkin and hollow it out. Fill it with the mousse and place it on a plate surrounded by gingersnap cookies.

You can also layer gingersnap cookies in a 9 x 9 inch pan and then add half the mousse, another layer of cookies and the rest of the mousse (sort of like banana cream pudding). Refrigerate it overnight before serving.

Banoffee Pie

Serves 6

This is my quick version of Banoffee Pie, which is an English pie that combines toffee, bananas and whipped cream. The traditional pie is incredible but very time consuming to make because you boil sweetened condensed milk in the can for hours until it transforms into "toffee." Instead, I boiled it on the stovetop and it took 15 minutes.

Traditionally, you'd make a homemade graham cracker crust, but again, you can shave a lot of time off with a store-bought one, which is what I used. As for the whipped cream, I used whipped topping, but this is good with real whipped cream, too.

This dessert is absolutely delectable, but it's rich so cut it in small slices.

The nice thing about this pie is you can take it to someone's house or a potluck and not have to worry about bringing home your dish because it's made in a store-bought graham cracker crust. It's also not a dessert you get every day, so people tend to love its uniqueness. Never underestimate the power of surprise when you're entertaining.

1 (9-inch) store-bought graham cracker crust

1 can sweetened condensed milk

1 tablespoon butter

1 (1.7-ounce) package of Rolo's

3-4 ripe bananas

2 cups whipped topping

Heath bar bits

In a small nonstick pot, combine sweetened condensed milk and butter and cook over medium heat for 10 minutes. Then add the Rolo's and continue to cook, stirring constantly, until mixture thickens, about 3-5 more minutes.

Pour into a pie shell and cool on counter for 10 minutes. Then refrigerate. When cool, slice 3 bananas and layer on pie. Topped with whipped topping. I use the last banana to add slices to the center of the pie.

Sprinkle Health bits around the edge of the pie before slicing.

Triple Strawberry Shortcake

Serves 8

I love this shortcake. Instead of just traditional whipped cream, I make strawberry cream and that always blows people away when they taste this.

The strawberry cream is a really a fruit dip my mom made for parties when I was growing up. It's so simple and was always a huge hit at her parties, so when I got older, I copied the idea for the dip but incorporated it into my shortcake.

I also use Red Top Oven Strawberry Jam which is some of the best local strawberry jam you can find in Springfield. Their products are available at the Farmers Market of the Ozarks (and other places); Red Top Oven in on Facebook where you can find all its sale locations.

You can taste the freshness of the berries in this jam. It's also on the thin side, so perfect for shortcake.

I call this a triple strawberry shortcake because it combines ripe Missouri strawberries; delicious strawberry jam and strawberry cream. It's delightful.

Tip: if you're looking for a fruit dip for a party or brunch, all you have to do is combine a jar of marshmallow cream with 8-ounces of softened strawberry cream cheese and serve it with strawberries, grapes and apples.

1 jar Red Top Oven Strawberry Jam

1 white cake made according to package directions or a store-bought angel cake (full size)

1 (8-ounce) package strawberry cream cheese, at room temperature.

1 (7-ounce) jar marshmallow cream

4 cups hulled, sliced Missouri strawberries (when in season)

1 (8-ounce) tub of extra creamy whipped topping to garnish

Bake a white cake according to package directions or use a store bought angel cake.

Slice and hull strawberries and set aside.

Mix together softened cream cheese (best to leave it out for an hour or more) and marshmallow cream until mixture is smooth. This will take 5 minutes.

To plate, cut a slice of cake and drizzle Red Top Oven strawberry jam on top. Top with ½ cup slice strawberries. *See photo on page 113.*

Put a huge dollop of strawberry cream on top of cake and serve with additional whipped topping.

Index

Appetizers..**9**

   Garden Vegetable, Dill, Chicken Flatbread..10

   Enchilada Dip 12

   Chilled Hot Wing Flatbread 15

   Southwest Egg Rolls 16

   Chicken, Bacon Pizza with Sundried Tomatoes.......................................18

   Mediterranean Quesadillas with Feta, Red Pepper Sauce.....................20

   Chicken Mole Bites...22

   Buffalo Chicken Pizza 23

   Creamy Gumbo Dip..24

Salads..**25**

   Southwest Quinoa Salad with Cumin-Lime Dressing 27

   Ode to Wine Country..28

   Chicken, Corn, Avocado and Black Bean Salad in Chipotle Dressing.....31

   Ultimate Classic Chicken Salad..32

   Asian Chicken Salad 34

   Barbecue Ranch Chicken Salad..37

   Hawaiian Chicken Salad..38

Soups **39**

   Slow Cooker Stock 40

   Traditional Stock 42

   Asian Stock 43

   Chicken and Dumpling Soup 44

   Light Chicken and Corn Chowder..46

   Vegetable, Barley and Chicken Soup...48

Chicken Pho...50

White Chili..51

Quick Posole 52

Chicken Tortilla Soup 54

Sandwiches **57**

Curried Chicken Salad...59

Chicken and Andouille Po' Boy with Horseradish Slaw 61

Gooey Chicken, Artichoke Sandwich 63

California Chicken Sandwich with Basil Mayo 64

Grilled Chicken, Ham, Arugula and Cranberry Sandwich 66

Chicken, Mushroom Tapenade Cheese Sandwich 68

Rosemary Chicken Salad...70

Light Greek Chicken Salad 72

Mock Muffuletta 74

Indian Inspired Pita 75

Main Courses...**77**

Chicken, Ranch, Black Bean Quesadilla 78

Lettuce Wraps with Sweet Peanut Sauce 81

Quick Chicken Marsala 83

Jordanian Inspired Chicken in Filo Dough 84

Southwest Style Stuffed Peppers...86

Puff Pastry filled with Chicken, Artichokes and Cheese 88

Barbecue Chicken Quesadillas with Corn and Bacon...........................90

Chicken, Bacon and Gorgonzola Flatbread...92

Creole Fried Rice 95

Goat Cheese, Chicken and Tri-Pepper Quesadilla 97

Mexican Lasagna 99

Moroccan Chicken with Couscous 101

BLT Alfredo 104

Chicken Pot Pie with Refrigerator Biscuits.. 106

Quick Chicken Enchiladas.. 108

Desserts **111**

Warm Chocolate, Peanut Butter Trifle.. 113

Pumpkin Butter Cheesecake 114

Lemon-Misu 116

Pina Colada Trifle (in honor of Uncle Floyd)....................................... 118

Five-minute Pumpkin Mousse 121

Banoffee Pie 122

Triple Strawberry Shortcake 123